STUDIES IN THE UK ECONOMY

Mrs Thatcher's economics:

Her legacy

David Smith

Economics Editor of
The Sunday Times

Series Editor
Bryan Hurl
Head of Economics, Harrow School

HEINEMANN
EDUCATIONAL

For my father

Heinemann Educational Books Ltd.
Halley Court, Jordan Hill, Oxford OX2 8EJ
OXFORD   LONDON   EDINBURGH   MADRID
ATHENS   BOLOGNA   PARIS   MELBOURNE
SYDNEY   AUCKLAND   SINGAPORE   TOKYO
IBADAN   NIAROBI   HARARE   GABORONE
PORTSMOUTH NH (USA)

© David Smith 1992

First published 1992

92 93 94 95 96 10 9 8 7 6 5 4 3 2 1

British Library Cataloguing in Publication Data

A catalogue record for this book is available from the British Library

ISBN 0 435 33018 7

Typeset and illustrated by Taurus Graphics, Abingdon, Oxon.

Printed and bound in Great Britain by Clays Ltd, St Ives plc.

Acknowledgements

Grateful thanks are due to my wife Jayne for her forbearance. Mention must also be made of my children Richard, Thomas and Emily, in spite of whom this was written. Thanks too to Bryan Hurl of Harrow School and Sue Walton and Rachel Houghton of Heinemann Educational, who acted as very capable midwifes on the project.

Thanks are due to the following for permission to reproduce copyright material:

Associated Examining Board for questions on pp. 16, 54, 72, 73 and 89; The Controller of Her Majesty's Stationery office for the tables on pp. 110, 17, 28, 49, 50, 51, 52, 66, and 68; for the graphs on pp. 19, 28, 55, 73, 74, and 89; for the charts on page pp. 55 and 56, and the extracts on pp. 1, 2, 8, 9, 10, 13, 23, 24, 30 and 31; *The Independent* Newspaper Ltd. for the cartoon by Chris Riddell on p. 89; Joint Matriculation Board for questions on p. 35; Oxford and Cambridge Schools Examination Board for the questions on pp. 35, 36, 37, 53, 54, 72, 73 and 89; Times Newspapers Ltd for figures on pp. 14, 32, 60, 61 and 76, and the article on p. 54; University of Cambridge Local Examination Syndicate for questions on pp. 16 and 89; University of London School Examinations Board for questions on pp. 16, 35, 53, and 89; University of Oxford Delegacy of Local Examinations for questions on pp. 16, 54, 73, and 89; Welsh Joint Education Committee for questions on p. 16.

The Publishers have made every attempt to contact the correct Copyright holders. If, however, any material has been incorrectly attributed, the Publishers would be happy to correct this at the earliest opportunity.

Contents

Preface		*iv*
Chapter One	An introduction to a changing economy	*1*
Chapter Two	Monetarism and the control of inflation	*3*
Chapter Three	Reining back the public sector	*18*
Chapter Four	Tax cuts and the supply side	*38*
Chapter Five	Union law and the labour market	*57*
Chapter Six	Mrs Thatcher's economic legacy	*75*
Chapter Seven	Conclusions	*90*
Index		*91*

Preface

Mrs Thatcher's economic policies have frequently caused heated debate and disagreement but whatever one's normative views, her economics cannot be ignored. To challenge them necessitates being informed. To support them requires judgement as to their successes and failures.

As a professional communicator David Smith has been well placed to study and explain these policies throughout Mrs Thatcher's terms in office and beyond, at a level which is appropriate for this series for schools and colleges. He charts the rise and fall of monetarism, the pursuit of the enterprise culture, people's capitalism, privatization and trade union reform. Here is both applied economics vibrant with its relevance, and economic theory combined with current living economics in the making.

Bryan Hurl
Series Editor

Chapter One

An introduction to a changing economy

The British economy underwent enormous change between the election of Mrs Margaret Thatcher as Prime Minister on 3 May 1979 and her departure at the end of November 1990. Some see that change as having been entirely for the good, with the elimination of inflation as a significant danger, the emergence of new attitudes in business and industry which brought rapid growth in productivity and a new mood of realism in industrial relations – in marked contrast with the spirit of self-destruction of the 1960s and 70s.

Critics of Mrs Thatcher and her government are, however, unwilling to accept the claimed benefits of the economic policies pursued after 1979. They are quick to cite the economic damage that those policies incurred. Thus, the critics say, low inflation was a worldwide phenomenon in which Britain was a lucky participant, and the low inflation of the 1980s was not sustained. High growth in productivity, or output per worker, is a temporary phenomenon brought about by the shedding of labour by industry on a massive scale; and high unemployment is the result of mistakenly harsh monetary and fiscal policies. Meanwhile, the critics say, the economy was kept afloat through the good fortune of possessing one non-renewable asset – North Sea Oil – and by the steady disposal of a limited stock of assets – state industries – by privatization.

Our task here is not primarily to take sides in this debate. The essential point is that no observer of the economic scene in Britain would dispute that the landscape has changed, in some cases beyond recognition. The period since 1979 has clearly been a very important one for economic policy. Some things have changed since Mrs Thatcher was replaced by John Major in 1990, but the broad thrust of economic policy is the same.

Four principles

Sir Geoffrey Howe, the first Chancellor of the Exchequer under Mrs Thatcher, set the scene for subsequent policy in his Budget speech on 12 June 1979: 'The British people are convinced, as we believe, that it is time for a new beginning,' he said. 'So our strategy to check Britain's long-term decline, which has gathered pace in the last five years, is based on four principles.' The Chancellor went on to list these

1

four principles as follows:

- to strengthen incentives by allowing people to keep more of what they earn, so that hard work, talent and ability are properly rewarded;
- to enlarge freedom of choice for the individual by reducing the role of the state;
- to reduce the burden of financing the public sector, so as to leave room for commerce and industry to prosper;
- to ensure, so far as is possible, that those who take part in collective bargaining understand the consequences of their actions (for that is the way to promote a proper sense of responsibility).

The Chancellor then added the following comment:

'These are simple principles, but they require substantial changes in the way our economy is allowed to work . . . . But they will not themselves be enough unless we also squeeze inflation out of the system. It is crucially important to re-establish sound money. We intend to achieve this through firm monetary discipline and fiscal policies consistent with it, including strict control over public expenditure.'

It is convenient, without departing from Sir Geoffrey's scheme too much, to examine Mrs Thatcher's economics in a slightly different order.

Mrs Thatcher's economics

I shall start with the purely *macroeconomic* aspects of economic policy, namely the goal of controlling and eventually eliminating inflation, principally though the control of the money supply. I then move on to an area that has both *macro- and microeconomic facets:* the policy of reducing the size and influence of the public sector.

The use of tax reductions as a means of improving incentives – that part of Mrs Thatcher's economic philosophy which is very much concerned with the supply side of the economy – comes next. Then I look at another area that is essentially microeconomic – the introduction of legislation both to curb the power of the trades unions and to improve the efficiency of the labour market.

These four elements of economic policy – monetarism and the control of inflation, reining back the public sector, tax cuts and the supply side, and union law and the labour market make up Mrs Thatcher's economics for the purpose of this book. Finally I examine Mrs Thatcher's legacy. Did she leave the economy in a better state than she found it? And how durable is the inheritance of 'Thatcherism', both in Britain and around the world?

Chapter Two
Monetarism and the control of inflation

'Under Labour prices have risen faster than at any peacetime period in the three centuries in which records have been kept, and inflation is now accelerating again. The pound today is worth less than half its 1974 value. On present form it would be halved in value yet again within eight years. Inflation on this scale has come near to destroying our political and social stability . . . . To master inflation, proper monetary discipline is essential, with publicly stated targets for the rate of growth of the money supply. At the same time, a gradual reduction in the size of the Government's borrowing requirement is also vital.' Conservative party manifesto, 1979

The belief that the key to controlling the rate at which prices rise in the economy lies in the control of the amount of money in circulation is based on one of the oldest ideas in economics. The **quantity theory of money** originated almost 300 years ago with John Locke and David Hume. It was modernized and refined by the modern quantity theorists, or **monetarists**, led by Professor Milton Friedman of the University of Chicago.

The quantity theory of money
In the eighteenth and nineteenth centuries, when the industrialized countries were gradually developing sophisticated banking systems and the use of paper currencies, the belief that prices could not rise without a prior increase in the quantity of money in circulation was the conventional view. It was not until the eve of the First World War, and the beginning of the end of the principle that all paper currencies were backed by gold, that the quantity theory was set down in a form recognizable to modern economists.

The Fisher equation
In 1911, Professor Irving Fisher of Yale University set down the following equation:

$$MV = PT,$$

where M is the quantity of *money* in the economy, V is the number of times it changes hands in a given period, or its **velocity of circulation,** P is the *price* level, and T is the number of *transactions,* again within a given period.

At first glance the equation seems to be indisputable: the quantity of money multiplied by the number of times that money is used to buy goods is just another way of describing the price of goods multiplied by the number sold. There is no way in which, barring leakages into and out of the economy, the two sides of the equation cannot be equal.

But V and T are strange animals. How do we know what they are? The answer, according to Fisher, was that the number of times money changes hands, V, was determined by factors such as the structure of the banking system and the frequency with which people are paid. It could be assumed to change very slowly, if at all.

Similarly, most pre-First World War economists did not feature unemployment in their scheme of things. Any surplus of labour would automatically be corrected by a fall in wages. It followed that, in conditions of **full employment,** the number of transactions was broadly constant over time.

This left the two remaining elements of the equation, M and P, which did change. Further, the quantity theorists thought it only sensible that changes in the quantity of money came before price changes: M determined P, or *increases in the quantity of money led to inflation.*

The Cambridge version

The Fisher equation left the quantity theory open to the charge that it did not prove that the link was from money to prices, and not vice versa. Could not rising prices call forth an increase in the quantity of money in a modern economy as people, realizing that goods were going to cost them more, increased their borrowing from the banks?

This criticism was tackled directly in the **Cambridge cash balance approach** to the quantity theory. This had M and P as before, but introduced two new concepts. The first, in place of T, was Y – the **national income** of the economy in real terms. National income, the sum of incomes in the economy, is equivalent to the amount of expenditure, or transactions. It is also equivalent to the amount of goods produced. Y is a wider concept than T, and easier to grasp.

The Cambridge economists believed that individuals wished to hold a certain proportion of their income in cash. This proportion they called k. Now, if there is sudden increase in the amount of money in circulation, people have more money than they wish to hold. They go out and spend. Under the classical assumption that real national income is at its full employment level, the effect of an increase in money is an increase in prices.

The Cambridge cash balance version of the quantity theory can be expressed as:

$$M = kPY,$$

where M is the quantity of money in circulation, κ is the proportion of income people wish to hold in cash, P is the price level and Y real national income. And the mechanism logically ran from money to prices.

Friedman's modern quantity theory

Finally, in the 1950s, Professor Milton Friedman further refined the quantity theory, and rehabilitated it after it had been discredited in the revolution in economic thinking led by John Maynard Keynes in the 1930s.

Keynes had said that the Cambridge view that people wish to hold a constant proportion of their income in cash was wrong, because the **demand for money** would vary according to the rate of interest. He postulated a speculative demand for money which was very sensitive to interest rates.

Friedman accepted that there were alternative assets that people might hold, and the interest-earning bonds cited by Keynes would be among them. He pointed out, however, that there was a far wider range of these assets than Keynes had allowed, including washing machines and houses.

The effect of an increase in money in circulation would be that people would start off with a lot of cash but would then move some of that cash into other assets – and not just financial assets such as bonds, but also goods. Thus the link from an increase in money to greater spending on goods, while slightly less direct, was as well established as in the Cambridge approach.

In Friedman's view, all the factors that made up the demand for money, including the rate of interest and the relative attractions of buying and owning goods, would tend to cancel each other out, leaving a stable demand for money.

'Stable demand for money' means the same as 'stable velocity of circulation', and this gives us the modern quantity theory of money:

$$MV = PY$$

where M is the stock of money, V is the income velocity of circulation (or the number of times a given amount of money changes hands as someone's income), P is the price level, and Y is real national income.

Unlike his predecessors, Friedman did not suggest that Y was unchanged at the full employment level of national income; when the stock of money changes, he said, it produces changes in both national income and prices. But the larger the increase in the stock of money, the more likely were its effects to show up in higher prices rather than higher economic growth. Friedman wrote in 1956:

> 'There is perhaps no other empirical relation in economics that has been observed to recur so uniformly under so wide a variety of circumstances as the relation between substantial changes in the stock of money and in prices; the one is invariably linked to the other and in the same direction; the uniformity is, I suspect, of the same order as many of the uniformities that form the basis of the physical sciences.'

The quantity theory in practice

When policy-makers take MV = PY as their basis, then the conduct of policy appears to be very straightforward. Suppose that the economy is growing by 3 per cent a year (in other words Y is rising by 3 per cent annually) but that inflation, the rate of change of the price level P, is an unacceptable 10 per cent. To reduce inflation to perhaps 5 per cent, action has to be taken to reduce the rate of growth of the money stock. In the case outlined above, the prescription would be to reduce the rise in the **money supply** from an existing rate of 13 per cent to something near to 8 per cent.

On the face of it this could hardly be simpler: set your target for the money supply and everything else falls into place. In practice, of course, things are rarely so simple.

What is money?

This sounds like a question hardly worth asking. But think about it for a moment: money is obviously the cash that you carry around in your pockets, but it is a lot of other things as well.

In a modern, credit economy, most people would take money to include cheques drawn on banks or building societies. They would also include overdraft facilities – automatic entitlements to borrow – including company overdrafts. And no modern definition of money, at least from the consumer's point of view, could possibly exclude those flexible friends, the plastic credit cards.

In Britain, at present, the Bank of England publishes statistics for a range of definitions of money, running from M0 through to M4. M0 is a **narrow mone**y measure, comprising notes and coins and balances held by the commercial banks at the Bank of England. It is therefore close to traditional definitions of money. M4 includes, as well as notes and coins, many other things, the most important of which are accounts held by people at banks and building societies. It is a **broad money** measure.

How do you control money?

There is more to money than the cash we carry around with us, and so there has to be more involved in controlling it than simply regulating the machines at the Royal Mint.

Monetary policy, that part of economic policy concerned with the availability of money and credit in the economy – has to try to do more than influence the number of £5 notes we carry in our wallets or purses; it has also to bear down upon the rate at which we write cheques or use our credit cards. (Fiscal policy, the other leg to economic policy concerned with taxation and public expenditure, is dealt with later in the book.)

Governments can seek to control the rate of growth of money and credit directly. **Credit controls** on 'hire purchase' were one example of this; the Supplementary Special Deposits Scheme, usually known as the **corset,** was another. (The latter restricted the rate at which the banks could increase their lending.) Both were abolished by Mrs Thatcher's government. Under present (1991) arrangements, the main way in which money and credit are controlled is through their price. The growth of money is controlled through the level of interest rates, as well as by the Government's influence on confidence and expectations in the economy.

As we shall see, controlling money with such a limited range of weapons is far from easy.

Will velocity be constant?

The essential assumption of practical monetarism is that the demand for money – and therefore the velocity of circulation – will be constant or move in a predictable way. If we think back to $MV = PY$, we can see what happens if V is not constant.

Suppose that, at the time the government is trying to achieve a reduction in inflation by slowing down the money supply, there is an increase in the velocity of circulation – each unit of money changes hands more frequently. It is easy to see why economic policy would be thwarted. The reduction in the rate of growth of M is compensated for by an increase in V. PY is left unchanged.

In the opposite situation, where the government is trying to ease monetary conditions by letting the money supply grow faster, in order to boost the economy, a reduction in the velocity of circulation would again upset things. The desired aim of increasing PY would be thwarted.

The stability or otherwise of the demand for money and velocity of circulation has been one of the battlegrounds between the Keynesian economists (the followers of Keynes) and the monetarists.

The Keynesians argued that demand and velocity were will-o'-the-wisps which shifted around frequently. The monetarists argued the case for stable and predictable money demand and velocity. Much of the hard evidence – and the experience of governments who have attempted to put monetarism into practice – suggests that the velocity of circulation is not stable.

This may not be too much of a problem, of course, if velocity is moving in a predictable way. This, too, does not often appear to be the case.

What about the real economy?

In the example outlined earlier of how a government would go about reducing the rate of inflation from 10 to 5 per cent by reducing money supply growth, it was assumed that this process would have no effect on the growth of real national income, which held steady at 3 per cent.

A tightening of monetary policy might, however, hit the real economy as much as it affected inflation. In the worse case, the reduction in the rate of growth of money from 13 to 8 per cent, as in the example, could leave inflation unchanged at 10 per cent and entirely impact on the real economy – turning growth of 3 per cent into recession where the economy is contracting by 2 per cent.

Monetarists recognized this possibility, although few were prepared for the dramatic economic slowdown that marked the earlier years of Mrs Thatcher's experiment with monetarism. Professor Milton Friedman gave evidence in 1980 to the Treasury and Civil Service Committee, a House of Commons committee which was conducting a special examination of monetary policy. He said:

> 'A successful policy of reducing inflation will have as an unavoidable side effect a temporary retardation in economic growth. However, continuation of the present level of inflation, and even more further acceleration of inflation, would at best postpone the retardation at the expense of a more severe retardation later.
>
> 'Past mistakes in economic policy have left us with no soft options. Our only real alternatives are to accept a temporary economic slowdown now as part of a programme for ending inflation, or to experience a more severe slowdown somewhat later as a result of continued or accelerated inflation.'

Timing problems

Monetarists have never claimed that the relationship between money and prices is a perfectly predictable one. Instead, there are said to be 'long and variable lags' between changes in the rate of growth of money and changes in economic growth and inflation (the gross domestic product in money terms).

Friedman, for example, found that the average time lag between peaks in the growth of money and peaks in economic activity was 16 months, but that this average was within a range from 6 to 29 months. In the opposite situation, a low point in money growth came, on average, 12 months ahead of a low point in economic activity. But here again the range was wide, from 4 to 22 months.

Therefore, monetarism could never be used with precision. Governments could not use monetarism for '**fine tuning**' the economy. This is why Friedman and other monetarists said that governments should adopt firm rules for the rate of growth of money, stick to them and, with a little patience, the beneficial results should come through. Clearly, this is easier for a theoretician to say than for a politician to accept.

Mrs Thatcher's monetarism

Mrs Thatcher's first government (in 1979) was not the first in Britain to operate targets for the money supply. Labour governments in the late 1960s and in the period 1976–79 had also sought to control the money supply within targets, at the insistence of the International Monetary Fund in Washington.

There have been three distinct phases to the monetarist experiment in Britain under Mrs Thatcher, beginning with something close to a textbook version of the theory, and gradually moving away from that.

Phase one: Rigid targets and the medium-term financial strategy

Mrs Thatcher's first government, unlike its predecessors, was ideologically committed to monetarism. Ministers believed not only that control of the money supply would squeeze inflation out of the system, but also that by publicly announcing **monetary targets** for the rate of growth of the money stock they would influence **inflationary expectations** in the economy, particularly in the crucial area of wage bargaining. The intention was set out clearly by the Treasury in its March 1980 Budget document:

> 'Control of the money supply will over a period of years reduce the rate of inflation. The speed with which inflation falls will depend crucially on

expectations both within the United Kingdom and overseas. It is to provide a firm basis for those expectations that the government has announced its firm commitment to a progressive reduction in money supply growth.'

The measure of money which the government chose to target was called **sterling M3**. It consisted of notes and coins and all sterling sight and time deposits with the banks, plus sterling certificates of deposit. The main elements within sterling M3 (now called plain M3) were cash and bank deposits. **Sight deposits** are those which are withdrawable on demand (in other words current accounts). **Time deposits** are those where notice has to be given to withdraw, or an interest penalty incurred, and are more generally known as deposit accounts. Sterling M3 was at the broad end of the spectrum of measures of money, described earlier.

In practical terms, controlling the sterling M3 measure of the money supply meant successfully restricting the growth of the two main counterparts of sterling M3, the public sector borrowing requirement (PSBR) and bank lending. The authors of Britain's monetarist strategy saw the control of the money supply and the PSBR as inextricably linked. The one could be used to strengthen the arguments for control of the other. It was thought that bank lending would be relatively easy to control, if interest rates were set at appropriate levels, and that the real difficulties would lie with the PSBR, because of the problems in controlling public expenditure. In the event, bank lending proved to be less responsive to interest rates than had been thought, partly because of **financial deregulation**, and it was this that caused most of the problems in achieving the sterling M3 targets.

In the first Budget of the Thatcher government, in June 1979, a one-year target was set for the growth of sterling M3. But the following March, with the launch of the **medium-term financial strategy**, a more ambitious four-year programme was set out, as shown in Table 1.

Table 1 The medium-term financial strategy

	1980–81	1981–82	1982–83	1983–84
Target growth rate sterling M3(%)	7–11	6–10	5–9	4–8
Actual growth rate(%)	17.9	13.6	11.7	8.2

(Source: HMSO)

The aim was to bring down the *rate of growth* of sterling M3 within a target range fixed for each financial year (the government's financial year runs from April to April). As the second line in the table shows, a reduction in sterling M3 growth was achieved, but the original targets were never actually hit.

The effect of the attempt to reduce money supply growth was, initially, to bring about the most severe British economic recession since the 1930s. This was not necessarily because the monetary targets were too tight – and even if they were the targets were not met. Rather, it was because of these two accompanying factors:

- the failure of wage settlements to come down quickly enough
- the sharp rise in the pound which was an important effect of the attempt to control the money supply.

The pay boom
The more slowly that expectations adjust in the economy to the idea of lower inflation, the greater the effect that controlling the money supply (M) is likely to have a real national income (Y) rather than on the price level (P).

In 1979 and 1980, when pay settlements should ideally have been moving sharply lower in line with the government's firm anti-inflationary resolve, they instead moved sharply higher. There were several reasons, some the fault of the government, some not.

As a backdrop, the Iranian revolution late in 1978 had produced the second sharp rise in world oil prices in a decade. This added to inflation and wage pressures in the UK.

Then, in the run-up to the 1979 General Election in May, Mrs Thatcher promised to honour the recommendations of a special commission set up to examine *public sector pay*. The Comparability Commission on Public Sector Pay, under Professor Hugh Clegg, recommended big increases, notably for low-paid workers in the public sector, and these set the tone for the 1979–80 wage round.

The June Budget then included a big increase in value-added tax (VAT), from rates of 8 and 12.5 per cent to a uniform 15 per cent. In addition, the Budget ushered in a period of high interest rates, which pushed mortgage rates up. Both produced a sharp increase in inflation, measured by the **retail prices index,** and this added to wage demands.

The government's stated aim of achieving a progressive reduction in money supply growth had little impact on wage bargainers. Trades union officials did not attach any credence to the government's monetary targets and carried on as before, for a time.

The strong pound
Most textbook monetarism was concerned with the theoretical world

of the closed economy, with no complications like overseas trade and the exchange rate. In 1979 and 1980 interest rates were pushed sharply higher to rein back the growth of the target money supply measure, sterling M3.

The effect of this, in combination with the boost provided by higher oil prices (because of North Sea oil the pound was now a **petro-currency**), was to push the pound sharply higher. In 1980–81 the pound reached the heights of $2.40–2.50 against the dollar, compared with a low point of just above $1.50 in the mid-1970s.

These factors, coupled with high wage settlements at home, made it virtually impossible for many British firms to compete either in domestic or in export markets.

Deep recession
The side effects of the initial monetarist experiment were dramatic. The economy fell into the deepest recession since the 1930s. Manufacturing output slumped 17.5 per cent between June 1979 and the spring of 1981. Unemployment rose to 3 million during 1982, from 1.2 million in 1979. It was in this context that the government embarked on the second phase of the British monetarist experiment.

Phase two: Pragmatic monetarism
When the government reviewed its record on the economy after two years in power, it was clear that the monetarist strategy, based on sterling M3, had run into difficulties. A new model was needed which would avoid the worst of the old and, in particular, the over-valued exchange rate.

The new model, formally launched in March 1982, was a reworked medium-term financial strategy. As well as setting targets for sterling M3, the government now brought in a narrow money measure, M1 (consisting mainly of notes and coins and bank current accounts), as well as a wider measure, PSL (private sector liquidity) 2, which was even broader than sterling M3, and included some building society accounts.

The old monetary targets were scrapped and new ones put in their place: 8–12 per cent for 1982–83, instead of 5–9 per cent, falling gradually to 6–10 per cent by 1984–85.

The tone of monetary policy shifted. No longer would everything be sacrificed in favour of hitting one particular target. Instead, policy would be conducted with rather more discretion than had been the case initially. A Bank of England official, John Fforde, described this change in 1982:

'As may now be visible, this means that setting objectives for the money supply, and endeavouring to carry them out, has become a more humble pursuit. It does not lack resolve, or a clear sense of direction, but it recognizes once more that the successful execution of monetary policy requires the exercise of judgement, and of a constantly interpretative approach to the evolving pattern of evidence. Except in some grave emergency, or in the initial phase of a novel strategy, the abandonment of judgement in favour of some simple, rigid, quantitative rule about the money supply does not reliably deliver acceptable results.'

Phase three: Pragmatism

The second phase of monetary policy lasted until January 1985, when the second of two sterling crises in six months had pushed the pound to within a whisker of one-to-one parity with the dollar. There was then a further policy shift.

In October 1985, sterling M3 was temporarily abandoned as a target. It was brought back in 1986 but finally abandoned completely in 1987. In March 1988, the Treasury said that more attention would be paid to the wider M4 measure than to M3. M4 includes building society as well as bank deposits. But the only money target was for the narrow money measure M0, and it was clear that domestic monetary targets would take second place to the exchange rate in the conduct of policy.

It was back to the familiar model of monetary policy of the 1950s and 60s, when interest rates were raised or lowered according to the strength of the pound. And it was no longer economic policy according to the quantity theory of money.

In October 1987 Nigel Lawson, Chancellor of the Exchequer since 1983, called (in a speech to the International Monetary Fund) for a permanent system of managed exchange rates for the major currencies. The replacement of monetary targets by exchange rate targets was almost complete. Three years later, in October 1990, the exchange rate target was formalized with Britain's entry into the **exchange rate mechanism** of the **European Monetary System** (see Chapter 6).

Why did inflation fall?

Britain's inflation rate, which reached 25 per cent in the mid 1970s and over 20 per cent in the early 1980s, averaged between 4 and 5 per cent in the period 1983 to 1987 (see Figure 1).

The description above suggests that the experience of Mrs Thatcher's governments with monetarism was of missed targets followed by a gradual shift away from rigid ideas about targeting the money supply.

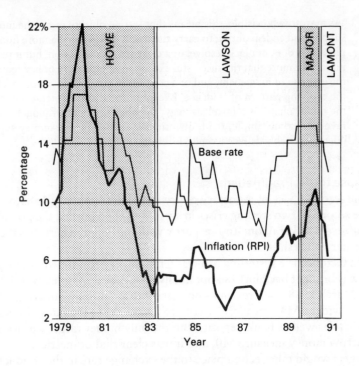

Figure 1 Interest rates and inflation (Source: *The Sunday Times*, 26 May 1991)

It does not read like an obvious success story, so why did inflation fall? There are several possible explanations.

Firstly, low inflation rates were achieved in the 1950s and 1960s without monetary targets. There is no reason to credit monetarism with that earlier success except insofar as the need to preserve fixed exchange rates (under the **Bretton Woods system** which lasted until 1973) may have exerted discipline in monetary policy. Low inflation occurred without monetarism then, so why not now?

Secondly, the two great inflationary surges of recent years – in the mid 1970s and around 1980 – followed sharp rises in world oil prices. For most of the 1980s oil and commodity prices were weak (the price of oil fell briefly to less than $10 a barrel in 1986) and this weakness exerted a downward influence on inflation.

Thirdly, recession and high unemployment have had a restraining influence on wage pressure in the major economies, although not enough to make major inroads into high unemployment levels.

Fourthly, fiscal policy – taxation and public expenditure – has been tightened in Britain, and in most other countries excepting the United States. Keynesian economists would say that this has been at least as important in producing low inflation as has monetary policy.

Finally, the re-emergence of inflation as a serious problem in the 1988–91 period demonstrated that Britain's monetarist experiment had not succeeded in one of its basic aims – that of destroying the inflationary psychology in the economy. Supporters of monetarism say that inflation's rise to a peak of 10.9% in the autumn of 1990 was due to the effective abandonment of money supply targets five years earlier. If, however, the earlier inflation fall was due to factors other than the success of the monetarist experiment, this explanation is open to serious doubt.

KEY WORDS

Quantity theory of money	Corset
Monetarists	Time lag
Fisher equation	Fine tuning
Velocity of circulation	Monetary targets
Full employment	Inflationary expectations
Cambridge cash balance approach	Sterling M3
	Sight deposits
National income	Time deposits
Demand for money	Financial deregulation
Money supply	Medium-term financial strategy
Narrow money	Retail prices index
Broad money	Petro-currency
Monetary policy	Bretton Woods system
Credit controls	Exchange rate mechanism
	European Monetary System

Reading list

Heathfield, D., *UK inflation*, Heinemann Educational, 1992.

Keegan, W., *Mrs Thatcher's economic experiment,* Penguin Books, 1984.

Morison, I. and Sheperdson, I., Chapter 4 in *Economics of the City*, Heinemann Educational, 1991.

Smith, D., *The rise and fall of monetarism,* Penguin Books, 1987.

Essay Topics

1. Explain why it is difficult to (a) define and (b) control the money supply. (Associated Examining Board, 1989)
2. What problems face the Bank of England in attempting to control the supply of money? (University of London School Examinations Board, 1990)
3. Why is bank lending an important factor determining the growth of the money supply? How does the Bank of England attempt to influence the volume of bank lending in practice in the UK? (Welsh Joint Education Committee, 1989)
4. Explain the main functions and official definitions of money. How does the government attempt to control the supply of money and what difficulties does it encounter in doing so? (University of Cambridge Local Examinations Syndicate, 1989)
5. What are the aims of monetary policy in the UK? How successful has monetary policy been in the UK in recent years? (University of Cambridge Local Examinations Syndicate, 1988)
6. Explain what is meant by a change in the value of money and consider how such changes are measured in practice. Consider whether the stability of the value of money over time ought to be a central objective of government macroeconomic policy. (Welsh Joint Education Committee, 1990)

Data Response Question 1
Growth of the UK economy between 1978 and 1987

The two tables opposite are based on information published in *Economic Trends*, 1988. All the figures, other than those for unemployment, are year-on-year percentage changes. The unemployment figures are percentages of the total labour force who are unemployed. Answer the following questions.

1. To what extent do the data in the tables support a monetary theory of inflation?
2. To what extent do the data support a demand-pull theory of inflation?
3. To what extent do the data support a cost-push theory of inflation?
4. How would you account for the course of inflation in the UK over this period?

(University of Oxford Delegacy of Local Examinations, 1989)

	Retail prices	Money stock (£M3)	GDP at factor cost at 1980 prices
	(per cent growth rate)		
1978	8.3	15.6	2.9
1979	13.4	13.2	2.7
1980	17.9	18.8	−2.3
1981	11.9	25.2	−0.9
1982	8.6	9.0	1.6
1983	4.6	11.2	3.3
1984	5.0	10.0	2.4
1985	6.1	13.4	3.6
1986	3.4	18.8	3.1
1987	4.2	21.8	4.3

	Unemployment rate	Average earnings (whole economy)	Output per person employed	Import prices (Unit value)
	(%)	*(per cent growth rate)*		
1978	4.7	N/A	2.7	3.6
1979	4.3	15.3	1.9	6.9
1980	5.4	11.9	−2.1	10.0
1981	8.5	12.9	2.0	8.2
1982	9.9	9.4	3.6	7.9
1983	10.7	8.4	3.9	9.3
1984	11.1	6.1	1.5	9.6
1985	11.3	8.5	2.1	3.9
1986	11.5	7.9	2.5	−7.7
1987	10.4	7.8	3.4	2.8

Chapter Three

Reining back the public sector

'*The state takes too much of the nation's income; its share must be steadily reduced. When it spends and borrows too much, taxes, prices and unemployment rise so that in the long run there is less wealth with which to improve our standard of living and our social services.*'
Conservative party manifesto, 1979

What is the right size for the public sector?

The term **public sector** is used so frequently that it seems hardly worth defining; but let us be clear what we are concerned with. The public sector consists of:

- all the people required to run government at both national and local level, and the resources at the disposal of those people;
- those services that are paid for out of taxation, including state education, the National Health Service, the police and the armed forces;
- the land and buildings owned by the government (public sector assets);
- state industries, whether or not they generate a profit.

Another way of distinguishing between public and private sectors is to draw the distinction between market and non-market activities. Government departments, state industries and the National Health Service are all in varying degrees insulated from the pressures of the market in a way that the bulk of private industry, for example, is not.

In the 1990–91 financial year, general government expenditure (excluding privatization proceeds) was 39.75 per cent of the country's gross domestic product, below the 44 per cent level inherited by Mrs Thatcher in 1979. In the intervening period, government spending rose and then fell as a proportion of gross domestic product (see Figure 2). The government intends to reduce the share to 39 per cent by 1993–94.

The difficulty is that there are no hard and fast rules about the right size for the public sector in a mixed economy such as that of Britain. (We call it a **mixed economy** because it consists of both public and

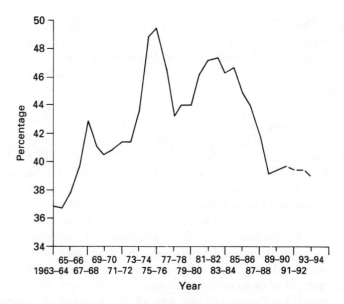

Figure 2 General government expenditure (excluding privatization proceeds) as a percentage of GDP (Source: The Treasury)

private sectors – it is neither 100 per cent free enterprise nor 100 per cent state-run).

In the mid-1970s, official figures were produced suggesting that public expenditure was equivalent to 60 per cent of Britain's gross domestic product. Warnings were sounded that a public sector of this size threatened not only the economic well-being of the country but her political and social stability. As it turned out the figures were misleading, involving elements of double counting: the actual figure was below 50 per cent. But the episode brought out deep-seated fears – even in a country with a well-developed welfare state – of too big a state sector. And the Thatcher government was able to advance a number of arguments for reining back the public sector.

Crowding out

The idea of crowding out had its ancestry in the so-called Treasury view of the 1920s and 30s, when successive British governments rejected the early ideas of Keynes about boosting public spending in order to reduce unemployment. Any increase in spending would require additional government borrowing, it was said. The pressure of such borrowing would push up interest rates and penalize private industry. The expansion of the public sector would thus be accompanied by a contraction in the private sector. The economy as a whole, and unemployment in particular, would be no better off.

Post-war economists refined this view into two distinct types of crowding out.

Resource crowding out

The resources of the economy are the factors of production – land, labour and capital – together with, according to the old classical economists, entrepreneurial ability. These resources are scarce. It follows that the greater the share of them taken up by the public sector, the less is available for the private sector.

One common reason advanced for Britain's long-run industrial decline was that the best talent from the schools and universities went, not into manufacturing industry where the financial rewards were often lower and the work less satisfying, but into the civil service. This was an example of resource crowding out.

Economists have criticized the use of the concept of resource crowding out when there are clearly unused resources in the economy – as, for example, at times of high unemployment. Even in such situations, though, it is still possible for there to be a limited supply of labour with certain skills. Even so, the reduction in the size of the civil service under Mrs Thatcher, and a perceived decline in the attractiveness of working in the public sector, have not solved manufacturing industry's problem. Now it loses much of the best young talent to the City and other private sector service occupations.

Financial crowding out

Advocates of the crowding out hypothesis would concede that there are certain situations when the scope for resource crowding out is limited; but, they would argue, financial crowding out can occur in a wider variety of situations.

Suppose that the government embarks on a programme of public expenditure which increases its annual borrowing (the **public sector borrowing requirement**) from £10 billion to £20 billion. The effect is to increase the amount of borrowing, whatever the rate of interest, by £10 billion. In Figure 3 the government's additional borrowing produces an outward shift in the demand for funds from D_1 to D_2. The effect, with the supply curve for funds unchanged (S), is to raise interest rates from R_1 to R_2, and to increase the amount borrowed from Q_1 to Q_2.

Now consider for a moment the private sector's demand for funds, as shown in Figure 4. The rise in interest rates from R_1 to R_2 would reduce

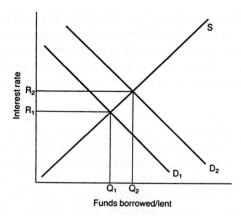

Figure 3 Borrowing and interest rates

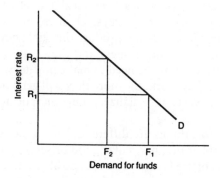

Figure 4 The private sector's demand for funds

the amount of funds demanded by the private sector – it would reduce private sector borrowing from F_1 to F_2. So it is possible that, if the extra borrowing by the public sector is exactly matched by reduced private sector borrowing, we would be back to our original demand schedule D_1 in Figure 3, with the important difference that a greater share of borrowing is by the public sector.

Critics of the financial crowding out argument say that the central idea of a finite amount of funds being available is not realistic. They also say that the rate of interest is only one of a number of factors determining private borrowing, and that raising interest rates has not proved to be an effective way of restraining borrowing. Companies borrow when they see investment opportunities, individuals when they are determined to purchase a house or consumer goods.

There have been occasions, however, when big increases in public borrowing have affected the interest rate *climate,* making it more difficult for private companies to raise finance in the City. And it is the case that around 80 per cent of daily stock exchange turnover is in government stocks (or **gilts** as they are more popularly known).

Public sector inefficiency

Even without resorting to the crowding out concept, free market economists can put forward a strong case for cutting back the public sector. The starting point for the argument is that the market exerts competitive pressures, which require economic units (firms) to operate efficiently. Without such competitive pressures there is no spur to efficiency. Hence the public sector, it is argued, will always tend to be less efficient than the private sector.

In the private sector, or at least an ideal model of it, spurs to efficiency work in a number of ways. Owners, managers and the workforce know that if they do not produce the right goods at the right price the firm will go out of business and they will lose their jobs. Managers are spurred on by the need to make profits; workers by the fact that the harder they work, the more they will get paid. Productivity is encouraged, waste is penalized, bureaucratic inefficiency is unforgivable.

In the public sector, things are different. The public sector body is the monopoly supplier of a particular good or service. The customer has to take what is offered because there is no alternative. There is job security for managers and the workforce. Even if the organization does badly it will not go out of business. Managers have insufficient reason to strive for greater efficiency because there is no reward for doing so – why rock the boat? Workers are paid the same, however hard they work. The scope for productivity gains is limited, the reward for such gains non-existent. Waste is not penalized, bureaucratic inefficiency is the norm.

Readers may have noticed that the above descriptions of the public and private sectors are caricatures. There are many private firms where the profit motive fails to permeate through to middle managers, and where the workforce does not link poor performance to the threat to job security. In the public sector, increased accountability and performance targets have allowed state bodies to match or improve upon private sector performance.

But the caricature is one that is widely believed, and the Conservative party had little difficulty selling it to the public.

Evidence for public and private sector efficiency

Comparisons of public and private sector performance are notoriously difficult. There is often little overlap between the services offered in the two. Where there is, one has to be sure that like is being compared with like.

Consider the National Health Service and private medicine. Private hospitals can offer an efficient service in conducting certain operations, without the problem of long waiting lists and bed shortages which are prevalent in the National Health Service. The NHS, on the other hand, is required to run a comprehensive service, available to all. Private hospitals are involved in only a part of the health-care market – you do not go to a private hospital for casualty treatment after a road accident. Private hospitals cater only for those who have had the foresight to take out private health insurance, or who can afford to pay. A poor, elderly person with a history of medical problems has to settle for the NHS – and it is in the necessary treatment of such patients that the costs of the NHS escalate.

Even without such problems in comparing services, there are still difficulties. All nurses and doctors in Britain are trained in the NHS. Most consultants have as their main job an NHS position. The NHS is generating what economists call **externalities** – wider social benefits – by training and providing the staff employed in private hospitals.

There are many other examples of externalities. Many of the well-paid economists in the City began their careers with the Treasury and the Bank of England. Their value in the private sector is enhanced because, having been involved in economic policy on the inside, they are better placed to assess policy from the outside.

In some cases, governments have required state industries or government departments to produce externalities explicitly by, for example, making them set up in areas of high unemployment. They may be made to lead the way in the employment of the disabled or racial minorities. This may not lead to inefficiency; but if it does it is the consequence of policy and not necessarily of the fact that the organization is in the public sector.

A study carried out by the economist Richard Pryke (consult the reading list) does paint a picture of public sector inefficiency. He analysed the performance of the main nationalized industries over the period 1968 to 1978 and concluded:

> 'The performance of the nationalized industries over the past decade has ranged from being good in parts – telecommunications and gas – to being almost wholly bad – BSC and postal services. Although the picture is not wholly black, most of the industries display serious inefficiency because

they do not use the minimum quantities of labour and capital to produce the goods and services that they provide. Furthermore, resources are being misallocated because of the widespread failure to pursue the optimum policies for pricing and production.'

He later compared the performance of specific parts of the public sector against private sector counterparts. Sealink, then part of British Rail, provided its services at a greater cost than Townsend Thoresen. The gas and electricity showrooms, measured in sales per square foot of floor space, did badly when set against Currys.

Results for other countries have been less clear-cut. In Canada, no significant productivity differences were detected between Canadian National, the public railway operator, and Canadian Pacific, a private firm. Similar inconclusive results emerged from comparisons in the Australian airline industry and US power supply.

Public and private monopolies

One of the commonest criticisms of **privatization** – the government's policy of transferring nationalized industries and other state assets and services to the private sector – is that it achieves nothing unless, in the case of monopolies such as gas and electricity supply, privatization also involves an injection of competition.

Critics of the policy (and British Telecom is the most criticized embodiment of that policy) say that **natural monopolies** can only be prevented from abusing their monopoly position when they are in state hands. Ministers can direct monolithic corporations on price, the standard of service, and so on.

The government would counter by saying that a properly regulated private monopoly will always be preferable to a public monopoly. Efficiency is forced upon the private monopoly by the need to perform for shareholders (and in the case of the privatized firms there are plenty of those). Meanwhile, regulatory watchdogs, with sharp teeth that are always ready to bite, provide safeguards against abuse.

Few would deny that the new private monopolies are good at generating profits. Arguments will continue to rage about whether the watchdogs – such as Oftel for British Telecom and Ofgas for British Gas – are effective.

The public sector burden

The greater the size of the public sector, the greater the amount of taxation or government borrowing that is needed to balance it. I shall examine the incentive effects of taxation in Chapter 4. The argument about restricting the size of the public sector to a level which can be met by taxation, without adversely affecting incentives, comes down to the fact that, ultimately, the wealth created in the private sector has to pay for the bulk of the public sector.

In the period 1976–78, the Labour government had to cut back sharply on public expenditure, after calling in the International Monetary Fund (**IMF**). The 1979 Conservative manifesto picked up on this and attacked Labour:

> 'By enlarging the role of the state and diminishing the role of the individual, they have crippled the enterprise and effort on which a prosperous country with improving social services depends.'

We come back to the question of what is the right size for the public sector. Clearly there is no easy answer. Furthermore it is no use specifying a fixed level for public spending as a proportion of gross domestic product for all time: that proportion should vary according to circumstances. Was there a case, for example, for running a larger public sector during the period of maximum production and tax revenues from Britain's North Sea oilfields?

A naturally increasing public sector?

I noted earlier that general government expenditure is currently running at about 39.75 per cent of gross domestic product. Public spending's share of the economy was high at over 45 per cent in the special conditions prevailing immediately after the Second World War. It dropped to more normal peacetime levels of 33–35 per cent in the 1950s, rising steadily to 40 per cent by the end of the 1960s. During the 1970s the share rose to over 45 per cent.

This increase was due to two factors. The first was the deliberate policy of improving public provision of services and, through nationalization, taking firms into public ownership. This was within the general policy context whereby public expenditure was used as a means of ensuring continued economic growth at times when private expenditure was weak.

The second reason related to the natural tendency for the public sector's share of the 'national cake' to increase. In a situation where productivity gains are concentrated in the private sector, the additional resources (wages, investment, etc.) allocated to the private sector will be partly offset by rising output per worker. In the public sector, where productivity gains are lower or impossible to measure, greater provision of services requires proportionately greater resources. Economists call this the **relative price effect**, and it occurs because the cost per unit of output of public services rises faster than that for private services and, therefore, of the overall price level for the economy. It follows that even the same amount of public services will require a rising share of private sector income to be taken up by taxation.

Therefore, governments have to take steps just to stop the public sector from increasing its relative size under its own steam. They have to take painful decisions on cutting public services or increasing public sector efficiency just to stand still in terms of the proportion of national income allocated to the public sector.

Public sector policy in practice – three phases of control

Just as monetary policy under Mrs Thatcher moved through three distinct stages, so a similar development has occurred with public expenditure. The three phases of control were:

- the initial attempt to put into force real (inflation-adjusted) reductions in the overall level of public spending;
- a revised policy of trying to hold public expenditure steady in real terms, implying a sharp fall in the proportion of GDP accounted for by public expenditure – as long as the rest of the economy was growing;
- a third phase which recognized that both the above aims were too ambitious.

Policy in the third phase attempted to ensure that real growth in public spending was below the growth rate in the economy as a whole. This, if successful, implies a gradual fall in public spending as a proportion of GDP.

Phase one: Real cuts

Mrs Thatcher's government was not the first to attempt to cut public expenditure. Governments had periodically resorted to cuts (which were often deferments of planned increases) as part of austerity packages over the years. The most notable example of this was the Labour government in 1976, under the influence of the IMF.

The Conservative government elected in 1979 was the first to aim for systematic real reductions in public expenditure over a period of years. The programme began almost immediately the government was elected and was formalized in the 1980 Public Expenditure White Paper.

The plans included a real increase in spending of just over 4 per cent for 1979–80, the government's first year in office. There were two reasons for this. By the time the government was elected in May, public spending for the 1979–80 year was in full swing. It is difficult to cut down on public spending during the year (the analogy is with turning round a supertanker) and the cuts had to wait until 1980–81.

The other reason was that during the election campaign the Conservatives made certain pledges that required an initial rise in public spending, notably the decision to honour the recommendations of a special commission under Professor Hugh Clegg for large increases in public sector pay.

'The government is determined not merely to halt the growth of public spending but progressively to reduce it,' the 1980 White Paper said. Within this overall reduction, however, there were major differences in the targets for individual areas of public spending.

Planned increases and planned cuts
There were, firstly those parts of public spending that the government wanted to increase quite sharply. Defence and law and order, both with double-figure percentage real increases over the four-year planning period, fell into this category, in line with pledges to boost spending on the police and the armed forces.

The second category of spending was where the government did not intend real cuts, but aimed to reduce growth sharply. It may come as a surprise to discover that the Conservatives did not intend cuts in the two most important areas of spending which fell into this category – the National Health Service and social security. It was the case for the social security budget, however, that the level of spending was planned to reach a plateau very quickly, and decline from that level.

The planned cuts in spending came in the third category and the list was a predictable one, including overseas aid, support for industry, lending to nationalized industries, education and the arts.

The cuts reflected the desire to increase private provision and reduce public provision. In the case of the arts, for example, private sponsorship was preferable to public subsidy. The housing budget would be sharply reduced, both by the sale of council houses to tenants and by a big reduction in the house-building programme.

Large-scale support and subsidy for industry had no place in Conservative free market philosophy. The Department of Industry's budget was cut. The nationalized industries were to be allowed to charge fair market prices for their services, with a corresponding reduction and eventual reversal of cash drain they imposed on central government.

Some of the planned cuts were very large indeed. The housing budget was to be virtually halved, and that for the Departments of Industry, Energy, Trade and Employment cut by over 40 per cent.

Cuts, what cuts?

The government's desire to cut public spending in real terms made itself felt in every office in every government department, and in schools, hospitals, university departments and other outposts of the public sector. Cuts there were. But the overall record of Mrs Thatcher's first four years was a large real increase in public spending, not a reduction.

Figure 5 tells the story. Had the government achieved its targets, the line would have gently declined from its 1979–80 peak. As we see, the line is undoubtedly rising. The plans, if achieved, would have meant a real fall of over 4 per cent in public spending between 1979–80 and 1983–84. In fact, there was a rise of about 7.5 per cent, not much lower than the 10 per cent increase planned by the previous Labour government over a similar period.

What went wrong? If we run through our three categories very quickly, it is easy to see. For the favoured areas of spending – defence and law and order – providing the extra resources promised turned out to require a lot more public expenditure than planned. This was particularly the case for defence, where the annual rise in the price of defence equipment bought by the services far outstripped the general rate of inflation in the economy.

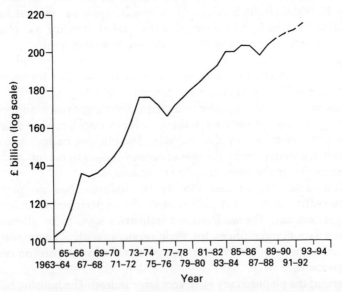

Figure 5 General government expenditure (excluding privatization proceeds) in real terms (Source: The Treasury)

In the second category – the big demand-led areas of public spending, health and social security – the government made the mistake of badly under-estimating demand. The rising real cost of health care was one factor, but more important was the impact of sharply rising unemployment on the social security budget.

Unemployment rose from 1.2 million when the Conservatives were elected in 1979 to 3 million by the end of 1982. Each additional unemployed person added just under £2000 to public spending, through the payment of benefits (the actual loss to the government was greater because of the loss of income tax revenue as people became unemployed). Unemployment may also have added to the pressures on public spending in other areas. For example, if unemployment leads to more illness among the population, the demands on the National Health Service are increased.

In the third category, where real cuts in spending were planned, the government failed through being too ambitious and through not taking account of the sharp downturn in the economy that occurred, partly because of world recession, partly as a result of the policy of trying to squeeze inflation out of the system. The best example was lending to the nationalized industries. In spite of the declared intention of making state industries pay their way, the government – and in particular Mrs Thatcher's first Secretary of State for Industry, Sir Keith Joseph – faced a stream of demands from these industries for extra funds, demands brought on by a combination of recession and large public sector pay increases.

In many cases these extra funds had to be provided as part of a programme of providing redundancy payments as these industries cut down on the number of workers employed. There were well-publicized battles between the unions and management of British Leyland. A long and expensive strike at the British Steel Corporation in 1980 was eventually resolved in favour of the management. The same occurred in 1984–85 with the National Coal Board. Recession and rationalization produced a sharp increase in the financial demands emanating from the nationalized industries.

Phase two: Consolidation

The depth of Britain's recession was reached in the spring of 1981. The public expenditure planning process in Britain, the Public Expenditure Survey and Control (**PESC**) round, begins in the spring when ministers submit bids for the following year's spending to the Treasury. These bids are examined in detail in negotiations over the summer between departmental and Treasury officials. In September, battle commences between the Chief Secretary to the Treasury (the minister in the Treasury responsible for spending, second in command to the Chancellor of the Exchequer) and the spending ministers.

Any outstanding disputes between departments and the Treasury (and there are usually plenty) are resolved by the co-called **star chamber** of senior ministers. If the spending ministers do not accept the verdict, the Prime Minister is the final arbiter. In November, the Treasury publishes its autumn statement, containing spending targets for the financial year beginning the following April.

There is still scope for further spending adjustment between the autumn statement and the Budget, which is usually in March. The whole process lasts for about a year. Between the Budgets of March 1981 and March 1982, the government's overall goal for public spending shifted from one of trying to secure a steady real reduction, to that of holding it constant in real terms.

This was still a considerable ambition. The recession of 1979–81 had ensured strongly rising public expenditure. As Peter Riddell observed in his book *The Thatcher Government* (Martin Robertson, 1983):

> 'Given the inherent upward pressures on expenditure on social security and the health service, the real question may be not why did public expenditure overshoot, but how did the government manage to contain the rise in the face of the deepest recession for fifty years? For example international figures compiled by the Organization for Economic Cooperation and Development show that public expenditure (after excluding transfer payments such as social security benefits) rose less in real terms in 1981 and 1982 in the UK than in any of the other big seven industrialized countries.'

The second phase of the public spending strategy, holding it constant in real terms, was no easy option. Although the emergence of the economy from recession eased the pressure on some of the demand-led areas of expenditure, the overall trend remained a rising one.

There were special factors such as the Falklands War, additional spending commitments ahead of the June 1983 election, and the 1984–85 miners' strike. But the overall message, which can be gleaned from Figure 5, is that public expenditure in Britain tends to rise by 1.5–2 per cent a year in real terms, come what may.

Phase three: Realism

This fact led to the third phase of the government's public spending strategy, that of allowing real increases but aiming to reduce the public expenditure share of GDP because the increases are smaller than those for the GDP. This was exemplified by the November 1986 autumn statement from the Treasury. It included big cash increases in spending: £4.7 billion in 1987–88 and £5.5 billion in 1988–89.

The extra spending was convenient in electoral terms, with a general election – won with a 100-seat majority by the Conservatives – held in June 1987. But it also reflected a new mood of realism on public spending – the official recognition that neither real cuts nor constant real spending could be achieved in practice. According to the Treasury:

'These plans mean that public spending is expected to fall as a proportion of the nation's income over the next three years. By 1989–90, the proportion is expected to be back to the levels of the early seventies. In real terms, public spending is expected to increase by an average of 1 per cent a year, significantly less than the growth of the nation's income.'

As it turned out, this third phase of public spending policy proved to be as difficult to achieve as its predecessors. Public expenditure's share of national income (general government expenditure excluding privatization proceeds as a percentage of GDP) rose in the four consecutive years 1988–89 to 1992–93.

Current and capital spending
One persistent criticism of the government's record on public spending has been that, while **current spending** by the government (on benefits, public sector pay, etc.) has increased, **capital spending** (public investment in new roads, hospitals and the rest) has been cut back.

The Confederation of British Industry has complained that cutbacks in this area have deprived industry of orders, while producing a crumbling **infrastructure** – with roads, public buildings and sewers falling into disrepair. The argument is not an easy one to resolve. The Treasury says that the maintenance of the infrastructure falls within current spending and any reductions in the capital budget are irrelevant to this question. The figures for capital spending are also affected by the transfer of public corporations to the private sector (whereupon their investment becomes private investment).

Privatization
The government has shifted its ground on public expenditure, and the results of policy were not as first intended. With privatization, however, the results as detailed in the following extract, have exceeded the expectations even of the optimists in the Conservative party:

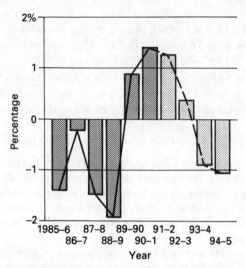

Figure 6 Public sector borrowing requirement as a percentage of GDP (Source: *The Sunday Times,* 24 March 1991)

'44 major businesses have been privatized ... Losses have been replaced by profits. In 1978–79 the nationalized industries which have been privatized received government subsidies of £19 million excluding capital grants and public dividend capital. By contrast, in 1989–90, those same companies, back in the private sector, contributed around £1,500 million to the Exchequer through Corporation Tax.

'Over 900,000 jobs have been transferred to the private sector. The sales themselves have produced £32.7 billion in proceeds for the nation. It is estimated that another £5.3 billion was raised in 1990–91. This money has helped the Government provide more resources for spending in priority areas such as health, while also allowing for repayment of substantial amounts of accumulated National Debt. Massive boost to share ownership. The number of individuals owning shares, even before electricity privatization, was 11 million – one in four of the adult population, and three times the number in 1979'. (Conservative Campaign Guide, 1991).

Privatization is the transfer of economic activity from the public to the private sector. It can be achieved by putting local authority refuse collection out to tender; or by allowing private bus companies to operate alongside state operators. But at its most dramatic it is the wholesale transfer of former nationalized industries into private ownership.

British Telecom used to be the telephones side of the Post Office. British Gas plc and Enterprise Oil were both part of the state-owned British Gas Corporation. Water, as well as the electricity generating and distribution companies, are in the private sector. Shares in British Petroleum and Cable & Wireless have been sold to eliminate the government's shareholding. The main airline in Britain, British Airways, has been sold off (as have the airports it and others use) through the flotation of the British Airports Authority. The National Freight Consortium is the largest employee buyout in the world. Britoil, Rolls-Royce, Associated British Ports, Amersham International, Jaguar and British Aerospace are all now quoted on the Stock Exchange as entirely private companies.

Privatization plays an important part in public finances. Sales of state assets count as **negative public spending**. As a result of privatization, the government currently has £5 billion a year more to use for spending or tax cuts than would otherwise be the case.

The sharp expansion of individual share ownership under the Conservatives would not have been possible without privatization. A survey published in 1987 by the Treasury and the Stock Exchange showed that share ownership increased from 7 per cent of the adult population in 1979 to nearly 20 per cent at the beginning of 1987, but that 8 per cent of the population held shares only in the privatized companies or the Trustee Savings Bank.

The government has instructed its financial advisers to market privatization issues heavily to the public. Attractive inducements to buy privatization shares, such as discount vouchers on gas and telephone bills, have been offered. The rationale is that the more people who own privatized shares, the greater will be the understanding of the need for profit in the economy, and the more difficult it will be for a future Labour government to take back privatized companies into public ownership.

Privatization, it is claimed, has sharply improved the performance of the former state industries, through the disciplines of the market. The government gains from the initial sale by raising money when such companies are floated. It also gains in the longer term, because these companies generate greater profits, part of which flow back to the government in the form of tax revenues.

The boards and managements of the former state corporations mostly prefer their new freedoms. They can raise money more easily on the capital markets, operate without having to refer to a sponsoring government department at every step, and pay themselves and their workers larger wage and salary increases.

Criticisms of privatization

There are plenty of criticisms of privatization, some of which can be summarized as follows:

- Privatization has simply transferred monopolies from the public to the private sector – it has produced no meaningful increase in competition.
- It has given people a distorted, 'casino' idea of share ownership, where instant gains can be made simply by subscribing to shares.
- The government has frittered away the proceeds of privatization in current public expenditure or tax cuts, rather than using them to improve the quality of the public sector capital stock – the infrastructure.
- The sale of the best parts of the public sector has left a rump of loss-making public corporations which will continue to be a drain on the Exchequer – their losses not offset by profits in other state-owned corporations.
- Privatization has deprived the government of the ability to use nationalized industries as a weapon of social policy – for example by creating employment in the depressed regions.

These criticisms do not alter the fact that it is with privatization rather than with the control of public expenditure that Mrs Thatcher's governments have been successful in reining back the public sector. And if the family silver has been sold, at least the new owners are keeping it well polished.

KEY WORDS

Public sector	IMF
Mixed economy	Relative price effect
Crowding out	PESC
Public sector borrowing requirement	Star chamber
	Current spending
Gilts	Capital spending
Externalities	Infrastructure
Privatization	Negative public spending
Natural monopoly	

Reading list

Bacon, R., and Eltis, W., *Britain's economic problem: too few producers,* Macmillan, 1976.

Hurl, B., *Privatization and the public sector,* 2nd edn, Heinemann Educational, 1992.

NIESR, *The UK economy*, Heinemann Educational, 1989.

Pryke, R., *The nationalised industries*, Martin Robertson, 1981.

Whynes, D., *Welfare State economics*, Heinemann Educational, 1992.

Essay topics

1. Why do economies have a public sector? Discuss how and why the size and composition of the public sector in Britain have changed in recent years. (Joint Matriculation Board, 1989)
2. What determines whether the UK has a public sector borrowing requirement or a public sector debt repayment? Discuss the likely economic consequences of the UK experiencing either a high PSBR or a high PSDR. (University of London School Examinations Board, 1990)
3. What have been the main trends in the composition of public expenditure over the last decade? Should the continuing growth of public expenditure be a source of concern? (Oxford & Cambridge Schools Examination Board, 1991)
4. Outline, briefly, the factors which can cause a market economy to fail to achieve an optimal allocation of resources. To what extent is the government's programme of privatization likely to improve the efficiency of resource allocation? (Joint Marticulation Board, 1988)
5. With reference to recent experience, examine the economic arguments for and against privatization. (University of London School Examinations Board, 1986)
6. Examine the arguments for and against a significant increase in public expenditure. (University of London School Examinations Board, 1986)

Data Response Question 2
Major tax receipts, borrowing and expenditure

The four tables overleaf are from *Barclays Bank Review*, May 1987. Study the tables and answer the following questions.

1. Define PSBR (Table A).
2. What are (i) public asset sales;
                 (ii) housing budget capital receipts?
   What is the significance of the term 'Underlying' PSBR in Table A?
3. Which items of public expenditure have grown fastest in real terms since 1979–80 (Tables B and C)? Account for the government's failure to reduce the level of public expenditure.
4. Why has the PSBR fallen as a proportion of GDP since 1979–80?

5. What are the implications of Table D for the government's economic strategy?

(Oxford & Cambridge Schools Examination Board, 1988)

Table A Public sector borrowing (£ million)

	1979–80	1986–87	1987–88 (Treasury forecast)
PSBR	10 020	3 333	3 900
Public asset sales	337	4 400	5 000
Housing budget capital receipts	472	1 886	1 702
'Underlying' PSBR	10 829	9 619	10 602
PSBR as % of GDP	4.8	0.9	0.9
'Underlying' PSBR as % of GDP	5.2	2.5	2.6

Table B Major categories of tax receipts at 1985–86 prices* (£ million)

	1979–80	1986–87 (estimate)	% change
Inland Revenue receipts	45 569	55 296	21.3
Customs and Excise receipts	29 485	40 039	35.8
National Insurance	24 254	25 753	6.2
Local Authority rates	11 168	15 063	34.9

*Adjusted using the GDP deflator

Table C Expenditure by department at 1985–86 prices* (£ million)

	1979–80	1986–87 (estimate)	% change
Planned expenditure on programmes, of which:	125 961	140 331	11.4
Defence	14 908	17 687	8.6
Education and Science	14 451	15 258	5.6
DHSS – health and personal social services	14 383	17 493	21.6
DHSS – social security	31 367	43 343	38.2

*Adjusted using the GDP deflator.

Table D General government receipts and expenditure (£ billion)

| | 1986–87 | | 1987–88 | |
	1986 budget forecast	1987 budget estimate	1987 budget forecast	% change
Total taxes and royalties of which:	117.9	119.4	127.8	7.0
Income Tax	38.7	38.4	40.0	4.2
Corporation Tax excluding North Sea	9.4	11.2	13.5	20.5
Value Added Tax	20.7	21.5	23.3	8.4
Local Authority rates	15.6	15.5	16.9	9.0
Other expenditure taxes	26.0	26.5	27.6	4.2
North Sea revenues	6.1	4.8	3.9	−18.8
National Insurance etc.	26.2	26.5	28.5	7.5
Other	11.5	11.7	11.8	0.9
General government receipts	155.6	157.6	168.1	6.7
General government expenditure	164.3	168.9	175.0	3.6

Chapter Four

Tax cuts and the supply side

'*We shall cut income tax at all levels to reward hard work,
responsibility and success; tackle the poverty trap; encourage saving
and the wider ownership of property; simplify taxes – like VAT; and
reduce tax bureaucracy.*

'*It is especially important to cut the absurdly high marginal rates of
tax both at the bottom and top of the income scale. It must pay a man
or woman significantly more to be in, rather than out of, work.
Raising tax thresholds will let the low-paid out of the tax net
altogether, and unemployment and short-term sickness benefit must
be brought into the computation of annual income.*

'*The top rate of income tax should be cut to the European average
and the higher tax bands widened.*' Conservative party manifesto,
1979

Direct and indirect taxation

Governments like to emphasize the taxes they plan to cut, and keep
quiet about those they are going to increase. The Conservative
manifesto held out the prospect of cuts in income tax – but an
important element of Conservative policy was not just reductions in
taxation but also a shift in the tax burden from direct to indirect
taxation.

Direct taxation, for individuals, consists of those taxes that are levied
directly on income. The main taxes in this category are therefore
income tax and national insurance contributions. Typically, income
tax is **progressive** in that the higher a person's income, the greater the
proportion of income taken in tax. This is achieved by having higher
marginal rates of income tax for higher income levels. (The **average
rate of income tax** is the amount you pay as a proportion of all
income, the **marginal rate** is the proportion taken in tax of each
additional pound of income.)

Unless they evade income tax (which is illegal) or employ financial
advisers to help avoid income tax (which is legal), people have to pay
it.

Indirect taxation for individuals consists of those taxes that are levied on spending. Value added tax (VAT) is the main one, together with the excise duties on, for example, alcohol, tobacco and petrol. Typically, such taxes are regressive, in that they are likely to take up a bigger proportion of a poor person's income than that of a rich person. A man earning £100 per week and smoking 20 cigarettes a day (leaving aside the question of whether he should be doing so) will pay the same amount of tax on his habit as a man earning £1000 a week and smoking the same amount. As a proportion of income, the poorer man is paying ten times as much.

There are ways of making indirect taxation less regressive – for example by setting higher rates of VAT on luxury goods such as caviar or silk shirts, or by setting zero rates of tax on basic necessities. In Britain, food and children's clothing are among the goods zero-rated for VAT purposes; but, unlike in some other EEC countries, there is no higher rate of VAT on luxuries.

The amount people pay in indirect taxation depends on what they spend. In an economy where all taxation was indirect, a rich person with basic needs would end up paying very little tax.

The 1979 Budget

The first Budget of Mrs Thatcher's government, presented by Sir Geoffrey Howe on 12 June 1979, contained a substantial shift from direct to indirect taxation. This was partly because the new government thought such a change desirable; and it was partly because the cuts in income tax it wanted had to be largely financed elsewhere in the tax system, if public borrowing was to be kept under control.

Before the June 1979 Budget, top-rate taxpayers faced a marginal rate of income tax of 83 per cent on earned income and 98 per cent on earned and unearned (investment) income together. In the Budget the top rate was reduced to 60 per cent, implying a sharp reduction in taxation for the richest people in the population.

There was also a big cut in the standard or basic rate of income tax – the marginal rate faced by the majority of the population – from 33 to 30 per cent. There was therefore a general reduction in income tax to accompany the cut in the top rates.

The other side of the coin came with changes in VAT introduced at the same time. Before the Budget there had been a standard rate of VAT of 8 per cent, which applied to the majority of goods on which VAT was levied (goods like food and children's clothing were and still are zero-rated for VAT purposes). There was also a higher rate of 12.5

per cent for some 'luxury' products. In the Budget these rates were increased to a uniform VAT rate of 15 per cent.

At Budget time, the Treasury provides estimates of the revenue effects of tax changes both for the forthcoming financial year (or in this case the financial year already in progress, 1979–80) and for a full year. The latter are the effects calculated on the basis that the new tax rates are in force for a whole year and are free of distortions such as spending ahead of VAT increases. The 1979 income tax reductions were calculated to have a full-year revenue cost of £4.5 billion. This was almost exactly offset by the VAT changes, which were reckoned to bring in an extra £4.2 billion.

Within these tax changes which were in overall terms, broadly **revenue-neutral**, there were important effects on the **distribution of income**. I noted earlier that indirect taxes are regressive: so with the extra VAT, paid by everyone from pensioners to millionaires, the extra burden on the pensioner, as a proportion of income, was much greater than that for the millionaire.

Taken in tandem with the fact that the biggest cuts in income tax were for the richest members of the population, this makes it clear that the effect of the June 1979 Budget was to shift the distribution of (post-tax) income in favour of the rich and away from the poor

Why cut income tax?

The 1979 Budget was the only example under Mrs Thatcher of a substantial shift from direct to indirect taxation, although the March 1991 Budget, shortly after her departure, also shifted from a direct tax (the Poll Tax) to an indirect one (VAT). The later emphasis was on cutting income tax, either through reductions in the basic rate of tax, or through raising the allowances and thresholds at which people begin to pay tax at different rates. In fact, as we shall see later, the overall tax burden faced by most people did not come down.

But why cut income tax? Apart from the political reason that if you give people tax handouts they are more likely to vote for you again (although opinion poll evidence has suggested a high level of cynicism among the British population about tax cuts), there are economic arguments for lowering income tax. They can be summarized as follows:

- Lower rates of income tax enhance incentives by allowing people to keep a greater proportion of the income they earn. People will work harder, spurred on by the knowledge that the extra money they earn is mainly for themselves, and not for the taxman.
- Income tax reductions – and in particular cuts in the higher rates of

tax – create an atmosphere in which enterprise flourishes. People will not bother to take the risk of setting up in business if they know that, even if successful, they will just end up paying more and more tax. Lower tax rates change all this.

- The lower the income tax rates, the less is the incentive for people to evade or avoid taxation. The unofficial **'black economy'** – the cash economy that goes on beyond the taxman's eye – has less reason to exist. People are less likely to take the risk of getting caught evading tax if the tax they would have to pay in the first instance seemed reasonable.

- The process of cutting income tax may have a beneficial effect on the rate at which pay is rising in the economy. Union representatives, knowing that their members are to receive a 'bonus' from tax cuts, may be less likely to push for big wage increases.

- Reductions in income tax, if properly implemented, can alleviate the **poverty trap**. The poverty trap exists for people on very low incomes. Their income is made up of earnings from work and from social security benefits. If their earnings increase, the social security benefits they receive are gradually withdrawn, because they are related to income. The situation can exist where a person on a low income simultaneously loses benefits and starts to pay income tax, with the consequence that the effective marginal rate of tax is very high, in some cases above 100 per cent.

- A related problem where income tax reductions could help is with the **unemployment trap**. A person who is unemployed and receiving benefits may find that after taking a job their net income actually falls, because income tax has to be paid on earnings. This problem is often characterized as the 'Why work?' syndrome.

Tax cuts and incentives

What determines how long or how hard people work? Economists usually start to answer this question by defining a trade-off, for individuals, between work and leisure. In such a model, work is unpleasant while leisure is pleasant. There is a trade-off between the two, work being necessary to pay for the enjoyment of leisure.

This trade-off can be expressed, as in Figure 7, in the form of an **indifference curve**. The individual is indifferent between high income and a small number of leisure hours, the opposite situation of low income and plenty of leisure, and points in between. Another line in Figure 7, budget line 1, relates hours of leisure to income – the greater the time spent in leisure the smaller the income. The optimum point is

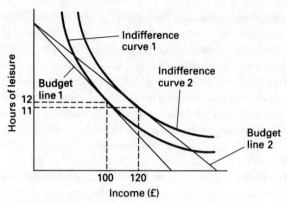

Figure 7 Indifference curves

reached when the indifference curve just touches the budget line, and this is the point at which the individual would choose to operate. He has a post-tax weekly income of £100 and enjoys 12 hours of leisure.

Now let us consider the effects of a cut in income tax. Our individual has worked out that, in order to pay for his leisure, he needs a certain fixed amount of post-tax income. A reduction in income tax increases post-tax income. The individual can afford to work fewer hours for the same take-home pay. This is a disincentive effect of lower taxation, and is known as the **income effect** of the tax change.

Furthermore there is another effect, the so-called **substitution effect**. A reduction in income tax means that leisure has become, in terms of income foregone, more expensive. The **opportunity** cost of leisure has increased because the post-tax income from each additional hour worked has risen. The substitution effect pulls in the opposite direction to the income effect – it provides an incentive to work longer hours.

In practice both income and substitution effects will appear, and the results of a cut in income tax are difficult to predict. In Figure 7 the effect of a tax cut is to produce a shift in the budget line to line 2 and a move to a new indifference curve (curve 2) outside the existing one. But the exact effect on the work/leisure trade-off will depend on the extent to which the tax cut has changed the *slope* of the budget line.

In our example, the effect of the tax cut is to increase the number of hours worked. The new intersection is at a daily number of 11 hours of leisure and a higher post-tax weekly income of £120.

Incentive effects in practice
The debate over the incentive effects of tax cuts has been a fierce one. Some economists say that tax cuts make no difference to how hard or

how long people work. Others say that incentive effects are very strong indeed.

A study commissioned by the Treasury, and carried out by a research team under Professor C.V. Brown of the University of Stirling, was published in 1987. It concluded, embarrassingly for the government, that cuts in income tax did not make people work longer hours, suggesting very weak incentive effects. Most employees, the study said, could not work any longer hours in their main job even if they wanted to. Some 79 per cent of employees were said to be restricted in this way. A 1991 study by the same author said that the 1988 cuts in higher rates of income tax had not made people work harder.

On the other hand, Professor P. Minford of the University of Liverpool, one of the leading lights of **supply-side economics** in Britain, says that cuts in tax rates motivate people to work and earn more to the extent that, following a cut in tax rates, tax revenues actually rise rather than fall.

A middle ground has been provided by the independent Institute for Fiscal Studies. It takes sides with the Brown study in that, in its view, only very large cuts in income tax would make any difference to the working behaviour of what has traditionally been regarded as the backbone of the workforce – prime-age married men. But the IFS believes – and its tax models support this view – that cuts in tax rates are important in encouraging married women to take jobs, or to work longer hours in existing jobs.

And certainly, between 1979 and 1991, the rise of over one million in the workforce in employment was more than accounted for by an increase in part-time jobs.

The Laffer curve

I referred above to Professor Minford's argument that lower tax rates, by boosting incentive, produce a net gain in tax revenues. This view was embodied in the **Laffer curve**, drawn up by an American supply-side economist Professor A. Laffer.

The Laffer curve is simple (see Figure 8). It starts by saying that there are two points – when the average tax rate is zero and when it is 100 per cent – when the government will receive no tax revenues. In the first case it is because no tax is levied. In the second it is because, if the average tax rate is 100 per cent, people are doing all their work for the taxman and it is not worth working.

Between these two points Laffer suggested, tax revenues will move in such a way that there comes a point when higher tax rates reduce tax revenues, because it is not worth working as much. And, looking at

43

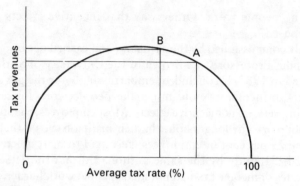

Figure 8 The Laffer curve

this the other way around, we can see the supply-side case for lowering tax rates.

Starting from position A in Figure 8, where tax rates are high, a reduction in rates could push us to position B, with lower rates but higher revenues. The government is then happy because it has gained both revenue and popularity. Individuals are happy because they face lower tax rates.

The Laffer curve has been strongly criticized. Indeed, even its creator has been reluctant to push it as a fully fledged theory. Critics say that even if one accepts Laffer's starting points, there is no evidence that the curve between those points runs in the way he suggested. There is also the criticism that Laffer's analysis is in terms of average tax rates and tells us little that is useful about marginal rates – and marginal rates are the ones that governments have to make decisions on.

Supply-side evidence

After cutting the basic rate of income tax from 29 to 27 per cent in his March 1987 Budget, the Chancellor of the Exchequer said: 'Lower rates of tax sharpen up incentives and stimulate enterprise, which in turn is the only route to better economic performance.'

In the testing ground of Mrs Thatcher's economic policies, there are two areas where, it is argued, this claim stands up. The first is the experience since 1979 for higher-rate tax-payers. In 1978–79, 24 per cent of income tax revenue was paid by the top 5 per cent of income earners. By 1991–92, in spite of the large 1979 and 1988 cuts in the higher rates of income tax, this proportion had risen to 32 per cent. Therefore, it is claimed, incentive effects have clearly worked. Enterprise, a proxy for which could be the increase in the number of higher-rate tax-payers, has flourished.

This argument is by no means clear-cut. It is challenged by economists who argue that the government's policies have produced a sharp shift in the distribution of income in favour of the rich, which has had little to do with enterprise. So a greater proportion of tax paid by the top 5 per cent may simply reflect greater *income inequality*, arising from very big income increases for the rich.

The second test case is not for individuals but for companies. In his 1984 Budget the Chancellor announced a *phased reduction* in the rate of **corporation tax** from 52 to 35 per cent. Alongside this, however, he announced the withdrawal of certain tax reliefs.

In the high-inflation 1970s, measures had been introduced to allow companies to offset against tax the rise in the value of their stocks which resulted simply from inflation. This stock appreciation relief was abolished in 1984. In addition, companies had been entitled to set outlays on capital equipment against tax, in order to encourage investment: up to 100 per cent of capital expenditure could be claimed against corporation tax in this way. The 1984 Budget announced the *phased abolition* of these capital allowances.

After the tax changes, which featured lower corporation tax rates, there was an increase in corporation tax revenues. In the years 1987–88, 1988–89 and 1990–91, a large rise in these revenues was partly responsible for the fact that the public sector borrowing requirement turned into a public sector debt repayment. Was this an example of companies striving harder to make profits because tax rates were reduced?

Again, the argument is not clear-cut. The Institute for Fiscal Studies said when the changes were introduced that the net effect of lower tax rates and the removal of tax reliefs was to increase companies' tax liabilities. The fact that the changes were followed by a period when, because of general conditions in the economy, company profits were in any case strong, means that the reduction in corporation tax rates cannot be held up as the only reason – or even the main reason – for higher corporation tax revenues.

The black economy

Where there is taxation there is also usually a black economy. The black economy (also known as the cash, hidden, shadow or underground economy) consists of activities carried out without officialdom – and in particular the taxman – knowing about them. Everyone knows of the tradesman who insists on cash-only payments, or the businessman who apparently gets everything paid for by his company, including his car, house and clothing.

Estimates of the size of the black economy vary. In Italy it is said to be the equivalent of one-third of the size of the officially recorded economy. In Britain, estimates range from about 3 per cent of national income up to 15 or 20 per cent. Sir William Pile, when chairman of the Inland Revenue, said that the black economy was equivalent to 7.5 per cent of national income. By its nature, no-one can tell the size of the black economy with any certainty.

If the black economy is regarded as a bad thing (and Sir Geoffrey Howe, Mrs Thatcher's first Chancellor, said that untaxed perks – one aspect of the black economy – were wasteful and divisive), then there are, broadly, two ways of reducing its size.

The first is to tighten up policing arrangements by increasing the number of tax inspectors, and to make penalties more severe. This has been done to an extent. Small businessmen complain of the attentions they receive from VAT inspectors. Income tax inspectors have become more vigilant when dealing with those occupations where the black economy is known to thrive.

The other route to killing off the black economy is to reduce taxation to levels at which it is not worth taking the risk of being caught evading tax, so more people opt for earning and paying tax legally.

The black economy is undoubtedly unfair in that the tax burden is unevenly shared. Some would say, however, that without the black economy things would operate less efficiently. (Anyone seeking to have building work done on a private house in the prosperous South East of England, for example, might find that they had to wait a very long time indeed if the black economy was entirely eliminated.) And it is doubtful whether tax cuts in themselves have much impact on the black economy: the taxation of perks such as company cars has made these less attractive than they were. Reductions in income tax are unlikely to make people switch in large numbers to the official economy.

The government set itself a target of reducing the basic rate of income tax to 25 per cent – a target achieved in the March 1988 Budget. That is still quite a high rate for someone who is of a mind to evade paying tax altogether. VAT, at 17.5 per cent, also provides an incentive for 'cash' payments for, amongst other things, building work. What is more, anyone declaring taxable income for the first time might have some difficulty explaining to the taxman about undeclared income in previous years.

The poverty trap
Consider the case of a low-paid family man who earns £100 a week in his job. In addition to this he receives £50 in social security benefits, because of the needs of his family.

Now suppose that his employer gives him a £20 a week pay increase. Will he be £20 a week better off? Probably not. The Department of Social Security will withdraw £20 of his £50 a week benefits, leaving him trapped on a weekly income of £150.

The position could be even worse than that. A man in his circumstances might be below the threshold at which income tax has to be paid on his original income of £100 a week, but the rise to £120 could put him in the position of having to pay tax. If he has to pay £5 a week in tax then the situation could arise whereby, as a result of the £20 a week increase, he ends up with an income from all sources of just £145. His effective marginal rate of tax – because of the simultaneous withdrawal of benefits and a move into tax-paying is *more* than 100 per cent. A pay increase of £20 has left him £5 a week worse off.

A reduction in tax rates would not help this family's plight very much; but an increase in the point at which the man starts to pay tax – by raising allowances and thresholds – could help to alleviate the problem. This was the method by which the government attempted to reduce the tax burden between 1980 and 1985.

Another development that has helped alleviate the worse features of the poverty trap has been to make all income – both taxes and benefits – subject to tax. The 1988 Fowler reforms of social security, with the new family income support, will also help get rid of the very high marginal rates of taxation/benefit withdrawal for those on low incomes.

The fact remains that, for many people on low incomes, only very large increases in earnings would allow them to break out of the poverty trap.

The unemployment trap

A close relative of the poverty trap is the unemployment trap. Returning to the example above, consider the situation in which our family man, instead of obtaining part of his income from work and part from the Department of Social Security, receives the entire £150 a week in the form of benefits. He is offered a job at £100 a week which, with the parallel withdrawal of some benefits, would leave his income unchanged at £150 a week. There is no *monetary* incentive for him to take this low-paid job, so he is trapped in unemployment.

Professor Minford of the University of Liverpool calculated that an unskilled family man would need to be paid £180 a week or more before it became worth while for him to take up employment.

There are two ways of tackling this problem. The 'stick' of threatening the removal of benefits if people do not take up work that is offered can be used instead of the 'carrot' of incentives for taking up a job.

Another suggestion has been the complete recasting of the income tax structure to include a **negative rate of income tax**. Under such a system, low-paid people would be on a negative rate of income tax – they would receive a payout from the government. As they moved up the income scale, this negative rate would decline until they reached the point at which they were paying normal, positive rates of income tax. Such a system, implying the integration of the tax and benefit systems, could ensure that incentives were part of the framework; but it still might not create much incentive to take up very low-paid jobs.

The threat of withdrawal of benefits – which the government applies to young people who do not take up employment or a Youth Training Scheme place – may sound draconian; but it *was* envisaged in the Beveridge Report as long ago as 1944. Sweden, which successfully pursued a full employment policy through the difficulties of the 1970s and 1980s, applies such rules.

Tax cuts and wages

The Conservative government has emphasized the growth in real wages as one factor contributing to high unemployment. Slower growth in wages (or even real wage reductions) would, it has been argued, reduce unemployment. This runs counter to the traditional Keynesian argument whereby reducing wages cuts demand in the economy and results in high unemployment.

The difficulty has been – with incomes policies having no place in the government's philosophy, and with such policies of questionable long-term effectiveness – how *do* you slow the growth in wages?

One suggestion is that income tax cuts, by automatically increasing take-home pay, may act as a dampener on excessive pay rises. A study in the National Institute *Economic Review* as long ago as 1976 found that tax cuts were the most effective weapon for governments wishing to reduce the rate of growth of wages. Other studies have found that the level of the **retention ratio** (the proportion of income that the employee takes home after tax) does not make much difference to pay rises. Therefore, the case seems to be made for a stream of tax reductions, each of which has an impact on a pay round.

The evidence during Mrs Thatcher's years in office for a slowdown in wages brought on by reductions in income tax rates is very thin. The tax cuts of the June 1979 Budget were followed by a sharp increase in wages, partly because cuts in income tax rates had been accompanied by higher VAT and a general upturn in inflation. The tax cuts of 1986 and 1987 had no noticeable impact on pay settlements.

In any case, the use of tax cuts in this way could only be a short-term palliative. Governments cannot, in practice, hope to cut taxes indefinitely. The solution to pay problems has to lie within the wage bargaining process itself.

The Thatcher record on tax cuts

In the twelve Budgets from 1979 to 1990, Mrs Thatcher's governments cut income tax in all except one. The exception was the austerity Budget of 1981.

In 1979, 1986, 1987 and 1988 there were cuts in income tax rates. In 1979 the top rate of income tax on earnings was reduced from 83 to 60 per cent and the basic rate from 33 to 30 per cent. In 1986 the basic rate was cut to 29 per cent, in 1987 to 27 per cent and in 1988 to 25 per cent. The government has set a target of reducing the basic rate to 20 per cent and in March 1988 reduced the top rate to 40 per cent.

In 1980, 1982, 1983, 1984, 1985, 1989 and 1990, as well as in some of the other years alongside rate cuts, tax allowances and thresholds were raised by more than inflation. This 'over-indexing' of allowances is simply another way of cutting tax, by moving the point at which people start paying tax. It was favoured as a way of taking people out of tax in the first half of the 1980s, partly because of its greater effect on the poverty and unemployment traps.

Income tax is not, however, the only direct tax that people pay. National Insurance contributions are also levied directly on income, and in some years these were increased at the same time as income tax was cut.

In his 1984 and 1989 Budgets the Chancellor of the Exchequer introduced measures to ease the burden of National Insurance on the lower paid, involving reduced rates for those on low earnings. Clearly, National Insurance has to be taken into account in assessing the government's tax-cutting record.

Tables 2–4 examine the tax positions of various income groups.

Three different points have been selected: immediately before the Conservative government took office (1978–79, five years through (1983–84), and Mrs Thatcher's last financial year (1990–91).

The tables give us the facts of changes in direct taxation under Mrs Thatcher. For the low paid (Table 2 shows those on 50 per cent of average earnings) the proportion of income taken by income tax and National Insurance contributions was higher in 1983–84 but lower by 1990–91 than in 1978–79. For a married couple with children there has been no reduction in the direct tax burden.

For those on average earnings (Table 3) the record for the first four years was poor, with the proportion of income taken in income tax

Table 2 Treasury figures for persons on 50 per cent of male average earnings (£154.45 a week in 1990–91)

	Single		Married with 2 children	
	£ per week	Per cent of gross income	£ per week	Per cent of gross income
1978–79				
Income Tax	7.91	17.0	3.26	6.3
National Insurance	3.02	6.6	3.02	5.9
Totals	10.93	23.6	6.28	12.2
1983–84				
Income Tax	15.35	18.0	9.53	9.8
National Insurance	7.70	9.0	7.70	7.9
Totals	23.05	27.0	17.23	17.7
1990–91				
Income Tax	24.04	15.6	1.27	0.8
National Insurance	10.64	6.9	10.64	6.9
Totals	34.68	22.5	11.91	7.7

Table 3 Treasury figures for persons on male average earnings (£308.90 a week in 1990–91)

	Single		Married with 2 children	
	£ per week	Per cent of gross income	£ per week	Per cent of gross income
1978–79				
Income Tax	23.22	25.0	18.46	18.8
National Insurance	6.03	6.5	6.03	6.2
Totals	29.25	31.5	24.49	25.0
1983–84				
Income Tax	41.00	24.6	35.18	19.2
National Insurance	15.39	9.0	15.39	8.4
Totals	56.39	33.6	50.57	27.6
1990–91				
Income Tax	62.53	20.3	39.76	12.9
National Insurance	24.49	8.0	24.49	8.0
Totals	87.02	28.3	64.25	20.9

and National Insurance contributions rising. Since then it has come down, and the direct tax burden for the 'typical' man on average earnings with two children was lower in 1990–91 than in 1978–79.

For the top earners (Table 4) the Conservatives' 1979 and 1988 Budgets provided a major boost. People in this category now pay a substantially smaller proportion of income in direct taxation than when Mrs Thatcher took office. People on above-average earnings paid about half their income in tax in 1978–79. Now it is just over a third.

Table 4   Treasury figures for persons on five times male average earnings (£1544.50 a week in 1990–91)

	Single		Married with 2 children	
	£ per week	Per cent of gross income	£ per week	Per cent of gross income
1978–79				
Income Tax	234.37	50.5	223.55	47.7
National Insurance	7.80	1.7	7.80	1.7
Totals	242.17	52.2	231.35	49.4
1983–84				
Income Tax	364.42	42.6	352.77	40.7
National Insurance	21.15	2.5	21.15	2.5
Totals	385.57	45.1	373.92	43.2
1990–91				
Income Tax	532.97	34.6	505.24	32.9
National Insurance	28.28	1.8	28.28	1.8
Totals	561.25	36.4	533.52	34.7

National Insurance, which is a very important factor in these calculations, is deducted from income at source for employees (not for the self-employed). As with income tax, the more you earn the more, in general, you pay.

However, there is a cut-off point for National Insurance above which contributions for employees do not increase. The upper earnings limit in 1990–91 was £390 a week. Thus, someone earning £600 or £1000 a week paid the same in National Insurance as a person on £390 a week.

The logic for this approach is that National Insurance payments are, as their name suggests, contributions to the National Insurance Fund.

If one takes the insurance analogy as appropriate, there is no reason why premiums should rise indefinitely with income. In practical terms, on the other hand, setting a limit for National Insurance contributions makes the tax system more regressive than it would otherwise be.

The general tax picture

I have so far discussed the government's record on direct taxation. What about the wider picture, taking in all forms of taxation? Have we become more or less taxed under Mrs Thatcher? Table 5 gives the picture for someone on average earnings and shows a slight fall in tax.

For the country as a whole the tax burden has undoubtedly increased. Comparative figures from the Organization for Economic Cooperation and Development show Britain to be roughly in the middle of the international league table on tax. But, as in most other countries, the overall tax burden has risen in recent years. Total taxation has risen from the equivalent of around 32.7 per cent of gross domestic product when Mrs Thatcher came to power in 1979, to 36.5 per cent in 1989.

Table 5 Total taxation, central and local government, for persons on average earnings (£308.90 a week in 1990–91)

| | Single | | Married with 2 children | |
	£ per week	Per cent of gross income	£ per week	Per cent of gross income
1978–79				
Income Tax	23.22	25.0	18.46	18.8
National Insurance	6.03	6.5	6.03	6.2
VAT	2.46	2.7	2.43	2.5
Other indirect taxes	7.54	8.1	7.91	8.1
Domestic rates	2.87	3.1	2.79	2.8
Totals	42.12	45.40	37.62	38.40
1990–91				
Income Tax	62.53	20.3	39.76	12.9
National Insurance	24.49	8.0	24.49	8.0
VAT	15.60	5.1	15.45	5.0
Other indirect taxes	21.50	7.0	21.99	7.1
Poll Tax	7.50	2.4	15.00	4.9
Totals	131.62	42.80	116.69	37.90

The government has set a target of reducing income tax further, taking the basic rate to 20 per cent. However, indirect tax has increased, with a rise in VAT to 17.5 per cent in 1991.

KEY WORDS

Direct taxation	Unemployment trap
Progressive	Indifference curve
Average rate of income tax	Income effect
Marginal rate	Substitution effect
Indirect taxation	Opportunity cost
Regressive	Supply-side economics
Revenue-neutral	Laffer curve
Distribution of income	Corporation tax
Black economy	Negative rate of income tax
Poverty trap	Retention ratio

Reading list

Armstrong, H. and Taylor, J., *Regional economics*, Heinemann Educational, 1992.

Glaister, K., *The entrepreneur*, Heinemann Educational, 1989.

Healey, N. and Levačić, R., *Supply side economics*, 2nd edn, Heinemann Educational, 1992.

Wilkinson, M., Chapters 6 and 7 in *Equity and efficiency*, Heinemann Educational, 1992.

Whyne, D., Chapter 3 in *Welfare State economics*, Heinemann Educational, 1992.

Essay Topics

1. Using economic analysis and relevant examples, discuss the relative merits and demerits of direct and indirect taxes. (University of London School Examinations Board, 1988)
2. 'The changes in income tax introduced by this government have had unfavourable economic and social effects.' Discuss. (Oxford & Cambridge Schools Examination Board, 1988)
3. 'A reduction in the benefits available under the welfare state is a reasonable price to pay for a further reduction in taxation.' Comment on this view. (Oxford & Cambridge Schools Examination Board, 1988)
4. Distinguish briefly between 'demand-side' and 'supply-side' economic policy. Should the government ignore the 'demand-side' and aim economic policy at improving 'supply-side' performance? (Associated Examining Board, 1988)
5. Discuss the role of fiscal policy in a modern economy, in both the

microeconomic and macroeconomic spheres. (University of Oxford Delegacy of Local Examinations, 1990)

6. What are the economic advantages and disadvantages associated with a reduction in the basic rate of income tax? (Oxford & Cambridge Schools Examination Board, 1988)

Data Response Question 3
Features of personal savings

The charts below are taken from *Economic Progress Report*, November/December 1986. Study them and then answer the following questions.

1. (i) Define 'personal sector saving ratio' (Chart 1).
   (ii) What factors might influence the size of the saving ratio?
2. What factors influence the relative shares of each of the items in Chart 2?
3. Is there a relationship between the trend in the personal sector saving ratio and the trend in inflation (Chart 1)?
4. What relationships between disposable incomes and saving are suggested by Chart 3?

(Oxford and Cambridge Schools Examination Board, 1988)

Chart 1 RPI and personal savings ratio

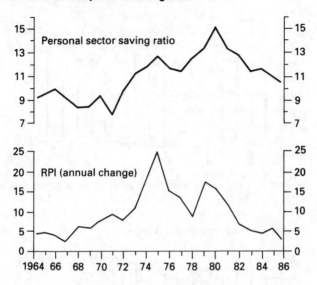

Chart 2 Allocation of personal sector savings

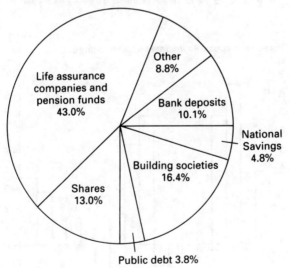

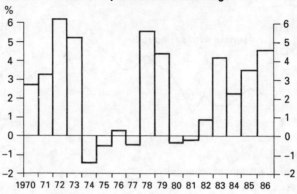

Chart 3 Consumer expenditure annual change

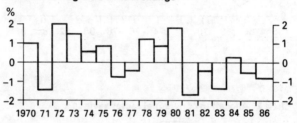

Personal saving ratio annual change

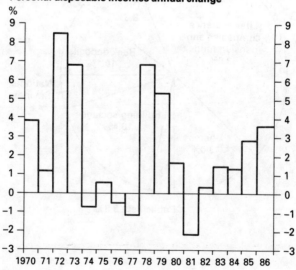

Personal disposable incomes annual change

Chapter Five

Union law and the labour market

'*A fair balance between the rights and obligations of unions, management and the community in which they work is essential to economic recovery. They should provide the stable conditions in which pay bargaining can take place as responsibly in Britain as it does in other countries.*

Free trade unions can only flourish in a free society. A strong and responsible trade union movement could play a big part in our economic recovery. We cannot go on, year after year, tearing ourselves apart in increasingly bitter and calamitous industrial disputes. In bringing about economic recovery, we should all be on the same side.' Conservative party manifesto, 1979

The role of the unions

Mass trade unionism developed in Britain in the second half of the nineteenth century. Unions were illegal until 1824 and grew only slowly, largely in craft occupations – skilled trades such as cutlery and furniture making – in the following 50 years. In 1870, well into Britain's industrial development, there were only about 500 000 union members.

From the end of the 1880s until the outbreak of the First World War in 1914, trade union membership grew rapidly, rising to about eight million. The chief cause was the spreading of unionization into non-craft occupations, and into the mass-employment industries such as road, rail and water transport and the iron and steel industries.

After the First World War the growth of the trade unions paralleled the emergence and growth of the Labour party. The General Strike of 1926 was a failure, but it was also a reminder of the potential force of organized labour.

For most of the twentieth century the trade unions have played a key role in the politics and economics of Britain, a role which has gone beyond that of simply representing their members in bargaining over pay and conditions.

The image of trade union leaders being invited to 10 Downing Street for beer and sandwiches has become a cliché; but it is indicative of a time, in the 1960s and 1970s, when governments could hardly make a move without the agreement of the powerful trade unions.

All this has changed. If Mrs Thatcher's aim was to reduce the power of the unions, then she and her government have certainly succeeded. In terms of power, influence and membership, the unions are but a shadow of their former selves. The role of the National Economic Development Council, which brought together the government, industry and the unions, has been scaled down. **Corporatism** – decision-making arrived at jointly by the powerful unions, the most influential industrialists and the government – is dead.

The interesting question is whether this has come about as a result of union reform or because of general economic conditions since 1979. I shall examine this a little later, but first let us look at some of the theory about trade unions and their effects.

Unions and pay

Figure 9 is a representation of the supply and demand for labour in an industry. We begin from a position where the industry is non-unionized. The supply of labour in this situation is represented by the line S_1. In the absence of unions, each worker is competing against all others. No one individual can threaten to withdraw his labour or someone else will take his job. There are no entry restrictions preventing people from working in the industry. There are, therefore, a large number of people willing to work at most wage rates. Higher wages do produce an increase in the supply of labour – more people are willing to work – but the supply curve is a gently sloping one.

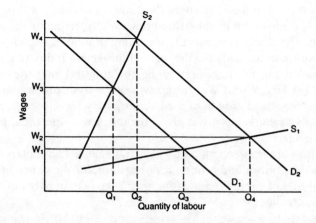

Figure 9 Labour supply and demand

The level of wages (W_1) is determined by the intersection of this supply curve (S_1) and the demand for labour (D_1), at which point the quantity of labour employed is Q_3.

uppose that, as a result of an increase in demand for the goods produced by the industry, extra workers are required at all wage rates. The demand for labour moves out to D_2. The effect is a small increase in wages, from W_1 to W_2, and a proportionately larger increase in the number of workers employed, from Q_3 to Q_4.

Now consider the position when the industry is unionized. The existence of the union has two principal effects. The first is to impose restrictions on entry by workers into the industry. In the extreme case, where all workers employed have to belong to the union (the industry **closed shop**), the union has ultimate control of the supply of labour. More generally, unions can insist on **entry restrictions** such as five-year apprenticeships to limit the supply of labour.

The other effect is to give workers as a whole the ultimate veto in wage bargaining. An individual worker can threaten to withdraw his labour, but it is an empty threat; the firm can carry on, other workers can be recruited. But when the union threatens to withdraw all labour at once, then the management has to take notice.

Returning to Figure 9, the effect of the union is to achieve a shift in the supply curve for labour. By exerting control over the number of workers entering the industry, and by bargaining collectively on wages, the union produces a much steeper supply curve (S_2).

In the initial situation, with demand D_1, the union attains a higher wage (W_3) but with a smaller number of workers employed (Q_1). When there is an outward shift in demand to D_2, there is a proportionately larger increase in wages (to W4) than in employment, which increases from Q_1 to Q_2.

The union mark-up

The above analysis suggests that unions achieve higher wages for their members, albeit at the expense of a lower overall level of employment within an industry. Most economists would accept that the principal role of unions is the achievement of higher wages.

Professor Minford of the University of Liverpool calculated that, over the period 1964–79, the union **mark-up** averaged 74 per cent. In other words, union members enjoyed wages 74 per cent higher on average than non-union members.

This comparison was, however, a very broad-brush one, essentially comparing unionized sectors of the economy with non-unionized sectors. Professor Minford described his comparison as between 'the unionized sector including its satellites and the non-unionized parts; think of mineworkers or firemen relative to cleaning ladies or Liverpool taxi drivers'.

Other estimates, based on jobs that are similar and comparing union and non-union wages, have found that a mark-up exists but a smaller one than suggested by Professor Minford. Work at the Institute for Employment Research at Warwick University found a mark–up which ranged from 1 per cent for skilled manual workers and 3 per cent for clerical workers, 4 per cent for middle managers and 10 per cent for semi-skilled manual workers.

If it is indeed the case that unions push up the wages of their members at the expense of employment, then an attack of union power should not result in higher unemployment. But in practice many unions did not conform to the theoretical model. Powerful unions and weak managements often resulted in a situation where the union could insist on both higher wages and higher employment. The high rates of pay and **overmanning** in the newspaper industry were a case in point.

Unions and employment (see Figures 10 and 11)

Union leaders would not admit that they bargain principally on pay and accept lower employment as a consequence. They would say that the more that trade unionism is spread over the economy, the greater is the dispersion of the twin benefits of high pay and high employment. Worker is not taking from worker, although workers as a whole may be claiming a bigger share of national income at the expense of profits.

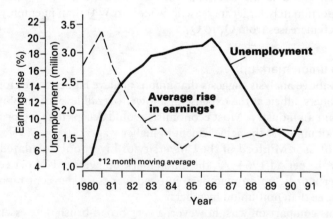

Figure 10   Jobs and pay (Source: *The Sunday Times,* 17 February 1991)

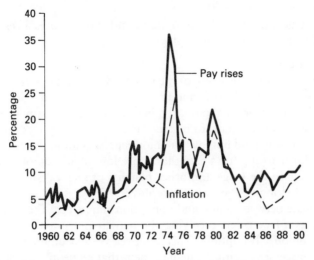

Figure 11 Pay and inflation (Source: *The Sunday Times*,
21 April 1991)

The experience of the 1980s provided a testing ground for the
motives of trade unions. During the 1979–81 recession – and
subsequently – there were many instances where the unions faced a
choice between accepting pay cuts for their members, or large-scale
redundancies. In all but a handful of cases the unions accepted
redundancies.

This experience tallies with theories of the labour market which
suggest that it is far from perfect in its operation. In the so-called
insider–outsider models of the labour market, there are two distinct
components of the labour force. The insiders are those people who are
in work, and probably represented by unions, or who are on the fringe
of work, having recently been in a job. The outsiders are those who
have been unemployed for a long time (for example a steelworker in
his fifties made redundant several years ago) or who have never
worked (for example the school leaver). These outsiders are not
represented in the labour market by the unions, and they are regarded
as disadvantaged by employers, because they do not have appropriate
skills or because their skills have gone rusty through lack of use.

It follows that the outsiders have very little influence on the labour
market – they could as well be in Australia for their influence on
Britain's labour market. While a relatively small increase in the
demand for labour could quickly absorb all those insiders who are on
the fringe of work, and then start pushing up wages, even a very large
increase in the demand for labour could leave the outsiders unaffected.
This is one reason why the government, along with others around the

world, targets its special employment and training measures at the young and the long-term unemployed.

Closed shops

Workers join unions because of the observed fact that union members – or at least those industries and firms that are unionized – apparently receive higher wages. (Apparently, because there are many instances where the opposite seems to be true. The financial services industry, 'the City', is well paid but low on union representation.)

A person working for a firm that is predominantly unionized can, however, gain the wage and other benefits of membership without actually belonging, because employers may not, in practice, discriminate between union and non-union employees. The individual can act as a **free rider**, receiving the benefits, essentially, of other people's union subscriptions. This is one reason why unions like closed shops – agreements with the management that all people employed in the firm should belong to a specified trade union. The other reason, of course, is that a closed shop provides unions with greater clout in negotiations.

Industrial action

The right to strike, for a worker to withdraw his or her labour over a grievance, is regarded as a fundamental one by most trade unionists. Employers often see things differently, regarding a strike as a breach of contract. It has long been the case in English law that the employers' interpretation of a strike as a breach of contract is the correct legal one, but for most of the post-war period until the 1980s few employers invoked the law in this context.

Industrial action can take forms other than strikes over a grievance affecting a particular group of workers. There can be, for example, an impasse in pay negotiations or a deterioration in working conditions, followed by industrial action which does not go as far as a strike – such as an overtime ban or a **work-to-rule**.

There is also industrial action that is not directly related to grievances with the employer. There may be political strikes, or action taken in sympathy with workers in entirely different firms or industries. This **secondary action** may also produce secondary picketing, when workers try to disrupt, not just the factory where the dispute began, but suppliers and customers of that factory.

Trade union reform under Mrs Thatcher

There were five main pieces of trade union legislation under Mrs Thatcher. The legislation was as follows.

The 1980 Employment Act

This Act gave employers the power to take legal action against secondary picketing – attempts to disrupt business away from the picket's own workplace. For example the electricity industry would be able to seek legal remedies against striking miners who tried to stop coal deliveries to power stations.

It also gave employers legal remedies against secondary industrial action – action not directly aimed at the employer involved in the industrial dispute. Again, the electricity industry would be entitled to take legal action against its employees if they had been persuaded by the coal miners not to handle coal at the power stations.

The right of unions to claim trade union recognition from employers was removed. Such recognition could still be claimed but without any statutory backing.

It was made easier for small businesses to dismiss workers without having to go through lengthy unfair dismissal proceedings.

The Act allowed people with conscientious objections to union membership or other strongly held views to opt out of union membership, even in closed shops.

Finally, the Act provided funding for **postal ballots** on industrial action or other matters. The aim was to produce a move away from the 'show of hands' method of deciding on industrial action, where individual union members could be pressured into voting for strikes even if they did not want them. As importantly, the move was seen as bringing about an improvement in trade union democracy, and a shift away from the situation in which militants achieved positions of power in the unions with ease.

The 1982 Employment Act

This Act made it possible for employers to take legal action against trade unions over industrial disruptions. Previously, action was only permitted against individual union organizers in firms.

Employers were given legal remedies against political strikes – those strikes where there is no dispute between employers and their own employees, or where the strike is not over employment matters. For example, employers could seek damages against workers taking part in 'days of action' over the banning of trade unions at the government's Communications Headquarters (GCHQ) at Cheltenham.

The Act introduced the protection of the law for all employees and for employers against closed shops that have not been approved by an overwhelming majority of the workforce. Further, it made contracts which specified 'union labour only' illegal.

The 1984 Trade Union Act

This legislation required elections to the executive positions within unions (that is senior trade union officials) to be by direct, secret ballot, normally by post.

It gave an additional incentive for the holding of strike ballots by means of secret voting. This would, henceforth, be a condition of the legal immunity of trade unions in organizing industrial action. Employers could sue for damages against strikes called without such a ballot.

The Act required unions to ballot their members every ten years on the continuation of political funds. (The majority of unions operate political funds and donate money to the Labour party.) This was seen as a potential weakening of the link between the trade union movement and Labour. Perhaps as importantly, it threatened Labour's long-term financial position.

Further union reforms

The government made it clear that it did not intend to let its push for union reform rest with the three Acts outlined above. In February 1987 it published a **Green Paper** (a discussion document on which comment is invited) called 'Trade unions and their members'. This contained a number of proposals which followed on from the earlier legislation:

- There was to be a further attempt to discourage closed shops by ending any legal protection for closed shops and making industrial action to enforce them unlawful.
- Members of unions were to be protected from disciplinary action by their unions if they refused to take part in industrial disputes.
- Strike ballots were to be given extra force by allowing union members to prevent unions from calling industrial action without a ballot, and requiring that the ballot must come out with a majority of members in favour before the industrial action goes ahead.
- Ballots for union executives were to be made fully postal and independently supervised and to apply to all union presidents and general secretaries.
- There were to be restrictions on the use of union funds – in particular, preventing funds being used in contravention of court orders. Union members were to be given the right to inspect union accounts.

- A new Commission for Union Affairs was to be set up to fund legal action by individuals or groups of union members against their unions.

The main provisions of the paper became law in May 1988, as the Employment Act 1988.

Finally, in the Employment Act 1990, individuals were given the right not to be refused employment on the grounds that they are, or are not, union members. They were also given the right to appeal to the Commissioner for the Rights of Trade Union Members for assistance in taking certain court action against trade unions. Employers were given the right to prevent industrial action which is intended to create or maintain a union closed shop.

Union membership statistics

Mrs Thatcher's success in her battle with the trade unions is, on the face of it, perfectly demonstrated by the fact that union membership has shown a marked decline during her time in office.

As Table 6 shows, 1979 was a watershed year for the trade union movement in two respects. Firstly, a government was elected which set out in a determined way to reduce union power. Secondly, Mrs Thatcher's election victory coincided with an all-time high for the number of union members, a level which will probably never again be reached.

Before investigating the subsequent sharp decline in union membership, let us look briefly in a little more detail at the union statistics contained in Table 6. Even at the 1989 figure of 309, which is 144 lower than ten years' earlier, there are a large number of unions in Britain. This has often been cited as a reason for Britain's lack of industrial success compared with countries like West Germany, which has a smaller number of unions and where one union per plant is the norm.

However, there are a large number of very small unions in Britain which are relatively unimportant in the overall picture. In 1989 there were 140 unions – nearly half the total – with fewer than 1000 members each; and these unions together accounted for only 0.3 per cent (35 000) of total union membership. By contrast, there were ten large unions with 250 000 members or more, which together accounted for 60.4 per cent of all union members. At the end of 1989, the biggest unions were: the Transport & General Workers' Union (1 270 776 members), GMB (823 176) the National and Local Government Officers Association (750 502), the Amalgamated Engineering Union (741 647), Manufacturing Science Finance

668 901), the National Union of Public Employees (604 912), the Union of Shop, Distributive and Allied Workers (375 891) and the Union of Construction, Allied Trades and Technicians (258 342).

Table 6 Figures for trade union numbers and membership

	Number of unions at end of year	Total membership at end of year (000)	Change in membership on previous year (%)
1975	470	12 026	–
1976	473	12 386	+3.0
1977	481	12 846	+3.7
1978	462	13 112	+2.1
1979	453	13 289	+1.3
1980	438	12 947	−2.6
1981	414	12 106	−6.5
1982	408	11 593	−4.2
1983	394	11 236	−3.1
1984	375	10 994	−2.2
1985	370	10 821	−1.6
1986	335	10 539	−2.6
1987	330	10 475	−0.6
1988	315	10 376	−0.9
1989	309	10 158	−2.1

Source: *Employment Gazette,* May 1991

Union membership tends to be most concentrated in manufacturing industry, mining, central and local government, the National Health Service, transport and public education. There is, by comparison, a much smaller proportion of union members in private sector service industries.

Why membership has declined
There are three principal reasons for the decline in union membership under Mrs Thatcher. The first, and most important, is the fall in employment in those industries where union representation has traditionally been strongest. Between June 1979 and December 1990, employment in manufacturing fell from 7.1 million to 4.97 million, a drop of over 2 million, a high proportion of which would have been trade union members.

The second reason has been the failure of the unions to make inroads into those sectors where employment is growing fastest. The unions have been slow to recruit in the service industries such as hamburger chains, or in fast-growing production industries such as electronics. Partly this has to do with the type of jobs on offer in the service industries. Much of the growth of employment in Britain since the employment trough of March 1983 has been for part-time workers, and notably for married women. When jobs are regarded as an opportunity for earning money on the side, there is very little incentive for the people who take them to join unions.

In addition, there has been a strong growth in self-employment, which rose by one million between 1983 and 1991. The unions have hardly gained a toehold among self-employed people.

The third factor – and the one which has been the least important so far but which is likely to grow in importance in the future – is the government's reform of the unions. Many people undoubtedly belonged to union because they had to – because they were working in a closed shop. The attack on the closed shop contained in the government's trade union legislation removes this reason for belonging to a union. And the overall reduction in union power and influence is likely to make more people think twice about joining or remaining members of unions.

Industrial disputes

One of the central aims of the Conservatives' trade union reforms was to achieve industrial peace. For many years the image of Britain was of a country beset with strikes and other industrial disputes, often over apparently trivial matters such as tea breaks. The strike weapon, it appeared, was used as a matter of course and not merely in the last resort.

A way of measuring the success of the reforms is, therefore, to look at the industrial relations record of Mrs Thatcher's governments compared with earlier periods (see Table 7). On the face of it the most recent figures – with days lost due to industrial disputes the lowest for 40 years – support the view that there has been a marked improvement in the industrial relations climate. But before jumping to this conclusion, we need to look at the figures in a little more detail.

Excluding 1979 – the figures for which were affected by public sector industrial disputes in the infamous 'winter of discontent', as well as a long engineering strike, largely before Mrs Thatcher took office – the record is an improved one. In the 1980–89 period an average of 7.4 million working days were lost a year because of industrial stoppages. This compared with 12.87 million days lost a year on average in the

1970s, a period notable for its industrial disruption. In the 1960s fewer than 5 million working days were lost annually.

The record is rather less impressive when two other factors are taken into account. These are the high level of unemployment under Mrs Thatcher and the growth in real wages.

Table 7 Figures for industrial stoppages

	Working days lost (000)	Working days lost per 1000 employees	Workers involved (000)	Number of stoppages
1966	2 398	103	544	1 951
1967	2 787	122	734	2 133
1968	4 690	207	2 258	2 390
1969	6 846	303	1 665	3 146
1970	10 980	489	1 801	3 943
1971	13 551	613	1 178	2 263
1972	23 909	1 081	1 734	2 530
1973	7 197	318	1 528	2 902
1974	14 750	647	1 626	2 946
1975	6 012	265	809	2 332
1976	3 284	146	668	2 034
1977	10 142	449	1 166	2 737
1978	9 405	413	1 041	2 498
1979	29 474	1 274	4 608	2 125
1980	11 964	521	834	1 348
1981	4 266	195	1 513	1 344
1982	5 313	249	2 103	1 538
1983	3 754	179	574	1 364
1984	27 135	1 280	1 464	1 221
1985	6 402	298	791	903
1986	1 920	89	720	1 074
1987	3 546	168	887	1 016
1988	3 702	170	790	781
1989	4 128	186	727	701
1990	1 895	85	293	611

Some small stoppages are excluded from these statistics
Source: *Employment Gazette,* August 1991

Mrs Thatcher inherited an unemployment level of 1.2 million. By the autumn of 1982 it rose to over 3 million, and subsequently reached 3.5 million. As I write this the level is 2.5 million, having fallen to 1.6 million in early 1990. It is still, by historical standards, very high. High unemployment, and the threat of redundancy and closure of firms, would normally be expected to act as a constraint on industrial action.

By the end of 1990 average earnings measured across the whole economy were 161 per cent higher than at the beginning of 1980. Prices over the same period increased by 106 per cent. The increase in real wages works out at 27 per cent, supporting the view that the unions did best at looking after those in work, to the detriment of the unemployed.

Most of these real wage increases, as some trade union officials have admitted, were easily won. They resulted, in part, from the fact that the inflation performance of the economy consistently came out better than wage bargainers had expected.

Again, large real wage increases would normally be associated with industrial peace. If workers are getting meaningful pay improvements then there should be less incentive for them to take industrial action.

The government would take issue with the charge that high unemployment has acted as a brake on industrial action. Many of the industrial disputes of recent years have been about redundancies and the slimming down of firms and industries – the 1984–85 miners' strike being the classic example. The backdrop of high unemployment, it can be argued, is likely to make unions fight even harder to preserve jobs in such situations, because if redundancies go through their members will have no other jobs to go to.

The government would also say that real wage rises have been earned through higher productivity (output per person employed). And the process of securing these gains in productivity, through changes in working practices and redundancies, has again involved industrial action.

The miners's strike and the Wapping dispute

Two industrial disputes under Mrs Thatcher have been seen as key developments in the history of the trade union movement. The first was the long miners' strike of 1984–85. At issue was the determination of the National Coal Board (now British Coal) to seek to close uneconomic pits. Two features of the bitter and often violent dispute over this issue stand out. The first was the failure of the National Union of Mineworkers to secure effective support from other trade unions. This may have been because other unions feared legal action under the Conservatives' trade union laws if they supported the miners. The second feature was that these laws, perhaps because the threat was enough, were not used to any great extent.

The defeat of the miners was mainly due to the sharp build-up of coal stocks at the power stations before the strike started. There was also a willingness to spend public money, notably on policing but also on allowing through larger pay settlements for other groups of public sector workers than might otherwise have been the case. The Chancellor of the Exchequer described this additional spending as a good investment.

The second key dispute was between News International and the print unions over a new plant at Wapping in East London. In January 1986, Rupert Murdoch announced his plans to produce a new London evening newspaper, the *London Post*, at Wapping. After failing to secure union representation on terms he could accept, the print unions announced their intention of taking industrial action. When Murdoch said that new contracts would apply throughout his existing titles (*The Sun, News of the World, The Times* and *The Sunday Times*) including a no-strike agreement, the print unions – the National Graphical Association and SOGAT 82 – called their members out on strike.

News International, using pre-Thatcher legislation, immediately dismissed the 5500 workers involved for breach of contract, scrapped plans for the *London Post,* and shifted production of the existing titles to the Wapping plant.

This time, the Conservative union laws were used, notably to prevent secondary industrial action. The print unions were prevented from calling out their members in other newspapers in sympathy, or from stopping their members handling News International titles at wholesalers.

This dispute continued into 1987 and was, at times, as bitter and violent as the miners' strike. But because the workers involved had been dismissed and because production of the newspapers continued, it did not feature in the statistics for days lost because of industrial disputes. Thus, the 1986 figures for industrial stoppages cannot be exactly equated with industrial peace.

The miners' strike and the Wapping dispute have left the unions in a weaker position. It now appears that determined employers, with the backing of the government, can defeat the big guns of the union movement. It is also the case that the two disputes have produced sharp divisions within the trade union movement. The National Union of Mineworkers remains in bitter conflict with the breakaway Union of Democratic Mineworkers. The traditional print unions, the NGA and SOGAT 82, are implacably opposed to the Electrical, Electronic, Telecommunication & Plumbing Union (EEPTU), which they see as having made inroads into printing jobs.

Unemployment and productivity

During the run-up to the 1987 general election, much was made of the transformation of the British economy, and of something approaching a British **productivity** miracle. There is a good deal of anecdotal evidence of new attitudes in Britain's factories and, indeed, of better productivity performance.

In the later part of 1987 and early in 1988, productivity in manufacturing industry, measured in terms of output per person employed, was rising at rates of 7 and 8 per cent a year – high by historical standards. The result was that pay increases, with average earnings in manufacturing growing by around 8.5 per cent, could largely be justified in terms of productivity improvements.

However, productivity growth tends to vary according to the position of the economy within the cycle. During strong periods of growth, productivity growth is rapid. When growth is weak, productivity slows. By the end of 1990, output per head in manufacturing was falling by 2 per cent a year, alongside 9.5 per cent earnings growth. Economists have agreed that there has been an improvement in productivity in the 1980s, but that the underlying rate of productivity growth in manufacturing – at around 4 per cent – has been well below average earnings increases. Thus, unless earnings growth slows markedly as economic growth moderates – which recent experience suggests it will not do – then there are potential problems for the economy in years to come.

It is important to remember when assessing the productivity improvements under Mrs Thatcher (and the frequently quoted evidence that Britain was at the bottom of the major countries' productivity league in the 1960s and 70s and at the top in the 80s) that there are two components to productivity growth. The two components of 'output per person employed' are output and employment. Productivity can increase simply by producing the same output with fewer people. This characterizes many of the productivity gains in manufacturing industry in Britain in the 1980s.

Between 1979 and the end of 1990, output per person employed in manufacturing in Britain rose by 50 per cent. There was an increase in manufacturing output over this period of 8 per cent.

The productivity improvement thus came mainly from the fact that 30 per cent of manufacturing jobs were lost over the period. In broad terms, in 1990 two workers were producing what it used to take three to do. This is a substantial gain in productivity, but arguably a less desirable one than when output is rising strongly and employment is stable, as appeared to be the case in 1987–88.

Some economists have questioned the extent of genuine productivity gains at the factory level. The 'batting average' view of productivity improvement is that it resulted from the closure of inefficient factories and not necessarily from productivity gains in the remaining ones, in the same way that leaving out the worst players from a cricket team would improve the batting average of those remaining.

For the economy as a whole the productivity gains of the 1980s have been rather less impressive than in manufacturing alone. The growth rate of output per person employed for the whole economy, which averaged 1.9 per cent over the 1980s period, has been no better than the long-run growth of productivity in Britain.

KEY WORDS

Corporatism	Industrial action
Closed shop	Work-to-rule
Entry restrictions	Secondary action
Mark-up	Postal ballots
Overmanning	Green Paper
Insider–outsider models	Productivity
Free rider	

Reading list

Clark, A. and Layard, R., *UK unemployment,* Heinemann Educational, 1989.

Healey, N. and Levačić, R., *Supply side economics*, 2nd edn, Heinemann Educational, 1992.

Morris, D. (ed.), *The economic system in the UK*, 3rd edn, Oxford University Press, 1985. Chapters 4 and 11 are relevant to this chapter, but the whole book can be recommended.

Essay topics

1. In the 1980s, both national output and the level of unemployment have risen in the UK. Examine the possible economic explanations of this phenomenon. (Associated Examining Board, 1987)
2. What have been the main changes in trade unions in the last decade? Why are there signs of recovery now? (Oxford & Cambridge Schools Examination Board, 1990)
3. What do you understand by 'full employment'? Critically discuss the view that full employment is no longer an achievable objective

of economic policy in the UK. (Associated Examining Board, 1988)
4. Does the experience of the 1980s show that the level of unemployment has no impact on the rate of inflation? (University of Oxford Delegacy of Local Examinations, 1987)
5. How are the level and structure of employment changing in the industrialized country you have been studying? (Oxford & Cambridge Schools Examination Board, 1988)

Data Response Question 4
Selected economic indicators

The charts below are taken from *Employment Gazette*, September 1989. Study them and answer the following questions.
1. Describe the trend in average earnings since 1980.
2. Account for the growing divergence between the output series and the output per person employed series after 1984.
3. Account for the volatility of input prices.
4. Why are the fluctuations in input prices not wholly reflected in output prices?
5. Use the data to account for movements in the RPI series since 1985. What other factors might have influenced the RPI over this period?
(Oxford and Cambridge Schools Examination Board, 1990)

Average earnings index — underlying (increase over previous year)

**Retail prices and producer prices
(input and output)
(changes over previous year)**

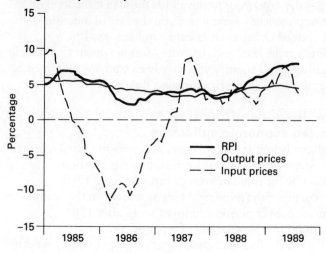

**Output and output per person employed
(changes over previous year, seasonally adjusted)**

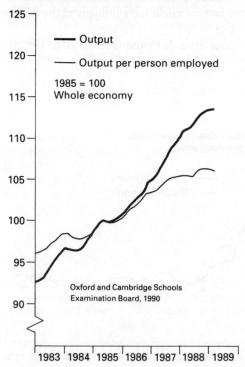

Oxford and Cambridge Schools
Examination Board, 1990

Chapter Six
Mrs Thatcher's economic legacy

"Thatcherism is not for a decade. It is for centuries' Mrs Thatcher,
Newsweek, 15 October 1990.

Margaret Thatcher stepped down as Prime Minister on 28 November
1990, having failed narrowly to retain the leadership of the
Conservative party in a ballot.

Economics propelled Mrs Thatcher to power. The 1978–79 winter
of industrial relations discontent, together with the widespread belief
that the Conservative party had something new to offer, provided the
basis for her first General Election victory in May 1979. Subsequently,
in 1983 and 1987, the achievement of low inflation and the return of
economic growth allowed her to remain in power. But economics, as
well as doubts over her style of leadership particularly in dealing with
the European Community, brought her down. When Mrs Thatcher
left office the inflation problem that she had prided herself on
defeating had come back. Inflation was at 10.9 per cent, its highest
since early 1982. The economy was in recession, brought on by more
than two years of high interest rates. From 5 October 1989 until
exactly a year later, bank base rates were at the historically high level
of 15 per cent. The new breed of home-owners, encouraged by the
government to buy their own properties, felt the pain of high interest
rates acutely. Unemployment, having fallen from mid-1986, began to
climb again in March 1990. A new form of local taxation, the
Community Charge or **'Poll Tax'**, had been introduced in Scotland in
April 1989 and in England and Wales in April 1990, amid widespread
protest. It was said to be the most unpopular tax in living memory,
and it was associated in the public mind, not with the individual
ministers who had introduced it, but with Mrs Thatcher herself. Less
than two months before she quit, Mrs Thatcher finally approved
Britain's entry into the **exchange rate mechanism** of the **European
Monetary System**. But hopes that this would provide her with a
political lifeline proved unfounded. It was to her successor, John
Major, who as chancellor had pressed strongly for ERM entry, that

75

she bequeathed the task of managing the economy within the new framework.

Assessing the Thatcher economic record

Mrs Thatcher's period in office lasted for $11\frac{1}{2}$ years (see Figure 12). She was Prime Minister for the whole of the 1980s. Over such a time-span there were bound to have been both successes and failures. How does one assess the record? My approach is a two-pronged one.

The first is to compare the record with the principles set out by Sir Geoffrey Howe in the June 1979 Budget, and described in Chapter 1 of this book. These were: to strengthen **incentives**; to reduce the role of the state; to reduce government borrowing; and to improve the framework of **collective bargaining** on pay, notably by restricting **union power**. All this was to be achieved under conditions of low inflation, themselves brought about by '**sound money**' policies.

The second line of attack is to analyse the Thatcher record on the basis of more conventional **economic indicators**: economic growth, productivity, investment, unemployment and the balance of payments. Of these I shall pay particular attention to the debate on the productivity 'miracle' and the significance of the deterioration in Britain's trade position under Mrs Thatcher.

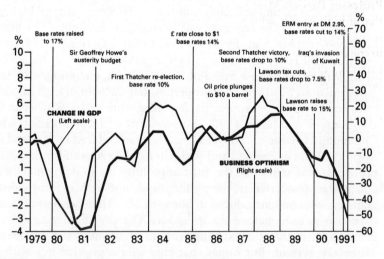

Figure 12 The business cycle in the Thatcher era (Source: *The Sunday Times*, 10 February 1991)

Incentives and the supply side

In May 1979 the top rate of tax on earned income was 83 per cent and the basic rate was 33 per cent. By November 1990 the top rate had come down to 40 per cent and the basic rate to 25 per cent. The record on income tax is, therefore, impressive. Another direct tax on individuals, however, National Insurance contributions, increased over this period, from 6.5 per cent of earnings to 9 per cent for most people. Even allowing for this, most people paid less tax as a proportion of their earnings in 1990 compared with 1979. Against this reduction in direct taxes, there were significant increases in indirect taxation. The Thatcher government took office when value-added tax (VAT) was at a standard rate of 8 per cent, with a higher rate for luxury goods of 12.5 per cent. In June 1979 the rate for all VAT-eligible products was increased to 15 per cent. In March 1991, four months after Mrs Thatcher's departure, the rate was increased further, to 17.5 per cent. *Taxes overall were not reduced in the 1980s.* Tax revenues as a proportion of gross domestic product averaged 37.4 per cent in the 1980–89 period, compared with 34.3 per cent for 1970–79.

Did income tax cuts, by improving incentives, make people work harder? Professor Chuck Brown of Stirling University, in two studies, suggested that the incentive effects of income tax cuts were insignificant. In some cases people actually worked less hard following reductions in the higher rates of tax because they could earn the same after-tax income as before, but with less effort. But calculations by Professor Patrick Minford of the University of Liverpool suggested that a high earner who had his tax rate cut from 60 to 40 per cent would work 15 per cent more hours. The Treasury pointed to the rise in the proportion of all income tax revenues emanating from higher rate taxpayers, in spite of the fact that the sharpest reductions had been in these higher rates, as proof that people had worked harder (or at least declared more income!) as a result of tax cuts. The debate is not easily won by either side. But one consequence of the Thatcher era is that high rates of income tax are no longer in fashion, and future governments will find it hard to introduce big tax increases.

Reducing the role of the state

Public expenditure policy evolved over the 1980s. The starting point was a policy of securing absolute reductions in spending. By the end, the aim was to allow growth in public spending, but to keep its growth rate below that of the rest of the economy. General government expenditure fell from 43.3 per cent of gross domestic product in the 1978–79 financial year to 38.8 per cent in 1989–90. Within the public expenditure total, the proportion spent on social security, health and law and order all recorded substantial increases. Most other categories of expenditure were stable, or fell significantly. The government's **privatization** programme was extensive and included the sale or transfer of British Gas, British Airways, British Telecom, Britoil, Enterprise Oil, the water industry, and the electricity generating and distribution companies. In all, well over £30 billion was raised from selling shares in former nationalized industries on the stock market. In addition, much of the council housing stock was sold to its former tenants, reducing the proportion of households living in properties owned by local authorities from 31.5 per cent in 1979 to 22.5 per cent in 1990. Other indicators are testimony to the reduced role of the public sector. Its share of the nation's capital stock fell from 44 per cent to under 31 per cent between 1979 and 1989; its share of employment dropped from 29.3 per cent to 23.1 per cent and its share of gross domestic product from 27.2 per cent to 20.3 per cent.

Under Mrs Thatcher, therefore, the role of the state in the economy was clearly reduced. The policy achieved its aims, but was it damaging to the economy? Critics say that the reduction was only achieved at the expense of a rundown in the nation's infrastructure, and a deterioration in the quality and availability of public services. Privatization, in turn, may have changed the ownership of certain industries, but it failed to introduce serious competition into these industries.

Reducing government borrowing

In 1978–79, the public sector borrowing requirement was 5 per cent of gross domestic product. Ten years later, in 1988–89, the public sector had a debt repayment equivalent to 3 per cent of gross domestic product. The **public sector borrowing requirement** (PSBR) had become a **public sector debt repayment** (PSDR). And, while the latter figure owed something to the unsustainable economic boom, and a little to privatization proceeds, a shift had plainly occurred. As this was being written, in the 1991–92 financial year, a public sector borrowing requirement of about 1 per cent of GDP appeared likely. In broad terms, and outside the exceptional circumstances of economic boom or **recession**, the public finances appeared to be in broad balance, with a long-run public sector borrowing requirement of zero, compared with typical PSBRs of 3, 4, 5 or more per cent of GDP in the 1970s.

The change was achieved by improved control over public expenditure under Mrs Thatcher, together with an increase in tax revenues as a share of GDP. But what did it achieve? Originally, the

Thatcher government set out to control public sector borrowing because of its importance as a counterpart to the sterling M3 measure of the money supply. When sterling M3 was abandoned as a monetary target, this role faded. More fundamentally, lower PSBRs were intended to prevent **financial crowding out** and, ultimately, to lead to lower interest rates than would otherside be the case. We cannot know what level of interest rates would have prevailed under a different path for the PSBR. But we do know that the average level of interest rates (bank base rates) under Mrs Thatcher exceeded 12 per cent – high in comparison with earlier periods. Thus, while public borrowing was clearly reduced the benefits of this success are harder to pinpoint.

Improving collective bargaining by restricting union power

When Mrs Thatcher came to power the labour market was inefficient, Britain was strike-prone and the unions, according to most assessments, had gained too much power. The most obvious successes of the government's union reforms were in the field of **industrial relations**. Although major employer–union battles were fought, the most notable being the battle between the National Coal Board and the National Union of Mineworkers in 1984, the general picture was of an improving industrial relations climate. By 1991, admittedly in a recession, days lost as a result of industrial disputes were running at their lowest level since the early 1950s. The British disease of a strike-prone workforce appeared to have been shrugged off.

Is Britain's labour market more efficient as a result? On one measure, the trade-off between inflation and unemployment, the 1980s were worse than in earlier periods. Throughout the Thatcher era, workers, or their union representatives, were unwilling to accept modest pay rises, even during a period of sharply rising unemployment. In the mid-1980s, unemployment climbed to well over three million but average earnings growth never fell below 7.5 per cent a year. Pay rigidities, shortages of skilled labour and the immobility of labour between regions and occupations were serious problems when Mrs Thatcher left office, just as they had been when she came to power.

Sound money and inflation

Mrs Thatcher entered office determined to master inflation and, for her first few years, she appeared to have succeeded. Inflation was 10.3 per cent in May 1979, rising to 21.9 per cent a year later. But by June 1983, and her second election victory, it was down to 3.7 per cent.

From June 1983 to June 1987, and her third victory, inflation reached a high of 7 per cent and a low of 2.4 per cent. At the time of the June 1987 election it was 4.2 per cent. After June 1987, however, things went wrong, the economic boom under the Chancellorship of Nigel Lawson culminating in an inflation rate of 10.9 per cent in the autumn of 1990, at the time when Mrs Thatcher stood down.

The record on inflation was, like the curate's egg, very good in parts. But it was not consistently good. Inflation rates vary from year to year, of course, even in the best-managed economies. But Britain's problem went a little deeper than that. The failure to achieve consistently low inflation owed much to the failure to maintain a consistent framework for monetary policy, which had been the intention in 1979. In addition, the inflation record was flattered by special factors. The initial sharp fall was largely as a result of the severity of the 1980–81 recession. In the mid-1980s all industrial countries benefited from low commodity prices and, in particular, a sharp fall in the world price of oil. As I write this towards the end of 1991, inflation is falling sharply in response to the severity of the 1990–91 recession.

Two views of the economy under Mrs Thatcher

Seldom has a Prime Minister brought out sharper divisions among economists than Mrs Thatcher. In 1981, 364 economists signed a letter criticizing her economic policies. But she also had her share of supporters. In assessing the record, it is instructive to look at the views of the two sides, beginning with **productivity**.

Productivity – the miracle

Professor Geoffrey Maynard of Reading University, in a paper entitled 'Britain's economic recovery' (see reading list), wrote that both labour and capital productivity rose impressively during the 1980s. Total factor productivity (capital and labour productivity together) rose by 3 per cent a year, the highest rate in the post-war period. Although part of this was due to the shake-out of labour, and the scrapping of inefficient capital, during the 1980–81 recession and its aftermath, the fact that it was sustained long after the recession suggests that something fundamental has changed. The record, writes Maynard, is even more impressive when set against other countries. In the 1960s, labour productivity (output per head) in manufacturing rose by 4.5 per cent a year in the seven major industrial countries (the United States, Japan, Germany, Britain, France, Italy and Canada), but by only 3 per cent a year in Britain. In the 1970s, the figures were 3.3 per cent a year for the seven, and only 1.6 per cent for Britain. In the 1980s the position was reversed. Labour productivity in manufacturing grew by 5.2 per cent a year in Britain, compared with 3.6 per cent for the Group of Seven (G7). In the 1980s, the growth of manufacturing productivity in Britain exceeded that of all the other G7 countries, including Japan. Taking all sectors of the economy, Britain's labour productivity growth grew by 2.5 per cent a year in the 1980s, compared with a G7 average of 1.8 per cent. Only Japan did better.

According to Maynard:

> 'It seems clear that an improvement in productivity which has been sustained for so long and shows every sign of continuing must be explained in terms of at least some of the longer term and fundamental factors typically underlying productivity growth: improved management, better working practices, better directed investment and greater readiness to change. The improved performance seems to be spread over most sectors of British manufacturing industry, being particularly marked in the metals, motor-car manufacturing and electrical engineering sectors of the economy.'

He received support from Kent Matthews of the University of Liverpool, in a paper called 'The UK economic renaissance' (see reading list). Matthews, quoting similar figures to those of Maynard, suggested that union reform and the more **deregulated economic environment** had been important factors in bringing about stronger growth in productivity in the 1980s. In addition, he wrote, income tax reductions had played a significant part. According to Matthews : 'The cut in top taxes has resulted in a renaissance in management.' The productivity improvement, on this view, has been driven by improvements on the **supply side** of the economy. Labour productivity has improved because people have been provided with incentives to work harder. Both capital and labour productivity have benefited from better and more motivated management.

Productivity – the mirage

Critics of the productivity miracle hypothesis accept, by and large, the figures described above. They ask, however, a slightly different question: if productivity growth has been so good, why have there not been more obvious benefits in overall economic performance?

Professor Wynne Godley of Cambridge, in a paper 'The British economy during the Thatcher era' (see reading list), writes that while Britain's productivity performance in manufacturing was 'outstandingly good' in the 1980s, it was not reflected in strong growth in manufacturing production, which was 'outstandingly poor'. During the period 1979–89, manufacturing output grew by only 1 per cent a year. He continues:

> 'Nor has the improvement in productivity brought any significant improvement in our ability to compete successfully in world markets, including our own. The volume of imports of manufactures nearly doubled between 1979 and 1988 whereas exports only went up about one-third. So the balance of trade in manufactures deteriorated from a surplus of about £3 billion in 1979 to a deficit of £14$\frac{1}{2}$ billion in 1988.'

Godley also cites the fact that, in spite of slow growth in manufacturing output, firms were reporting capacity constraints and skill shortages by 1988. Thus, improved productivity growth had not established a sustainable basis for an expansion in manufacturing output.

John Wells, also of Cambridge, in a paper 'The economy after ten years: stronger or weaker?' (see reading list), supports Godley's view. Wells also makes the point that British manufacturers have conceded a lot of ground to importers during the 1980s. In addition, he writes, firms failed to translate increases in labour productivity and profitability into higher investment. Only in 1988 did manufacturing investment, at constant prices, rise above its level in the late 1970s. The principal reason for this, he suggests, is that British companies have changed their strategy. The impressive growth in productivity has been across a smaller and more specialized product range. He writes:

> 'There is a growing body of evidence that many UK manufacturers have decided to opt for "niche" strategies. Having conceded certain mass markets for standardized commodities, both at home and abroad, to their competitors, they have decided to concentrate on smaller, more specialised, possibly high-profit activities – a strategy that guarantees a company a quite viable and profitable existence but does not result in the recapturing of mass markets at home or abroad.'

A long-term balance of payments problem

In 1979 Britain had a small current account deficit of £453 million. Ten years later in 1989, Mrs Thatcher's last full year in office, the deficit was £19.1 billion, more than 40 times as large. Critics of Mrs Thatcher's governments say that this underlines the weakness of the economy's performance during the period. Professor Godley says that one of the most alarming features of Britain's economic recovery in the

1980s was the rapid increase in imports. Imports as a proportion of gross domestic product rose from 29 per cent in 1981 to 37 per cent in 1988. He writes:

'It is the rapid growth of import penetration relative to exports which means that the expansion of the economy cannot now be sustained and which therefore poses colossal strategic problems for the future.'

John Wells agrees. He says that the failure of policy in the 1980s was that **internal balance** (full employment and stable prices) could not be combined with **external balance** (the current account together with long-term capital movements). This, he says, is because Britain's manufacturing sector has been allowed to become too small. He writes:

'Britain simply does not have a large enough manufacturing sector to sustain the level of total domestic expenditure on traded and non-traded goods and services alike that would be associated with full employment.'

The composition of the balance of payments tells us something about where the problem lies. From 1979 until the mid-1980s, Britain's trade in oil moved sharply into surplus, as oil exports from the North Sea increased. By 1985, the surplus on oil trade (just £300 million in 1980) was £8.1 billion, and the current account was in surplus by £2.7 billion. Since then, however, because of declining oil production and prices, the oil surplus has fallen, to £1.3 billion in 1989 and £1.6 billion in 1990. Meanwhile, there has been a rising deficit on non-oil trade – food, raw materials and, increasingly, manufactured goods. In 1980, Britain had a surplus of £1 billion on non-oil trade but by 1985 non-oil trade was in deficit by £11.4 billion. By 1989 this deficit was £25.3 billion, although it fell to £19.5 billion in 1990. The trade position in manufactures, in surplus by £6.4 billion in 1980, had shifted to a deficit of £3.8 billion by 1985 and £17.2 billion in 1989, although again it narrowed to £9.4 billion in 1990. The final element in the current account equation is the trade in invisible goods – services such as tourism, shipping, banking and insurance, together with interest, profits, dividends and transfers. In 1986 the invisibles surplus reached a peak of £9.5 billion. By 1990, however, this had halved to £4.7 billion. The three elements of the **current account** – a rising non-oil trade deficit, a decline in the oil surplus and a fall in the invisibles surplus – all served to increase the current account deficit in the second half of the 1980s. Critics of Mrs Thatcher and her policies believe that these trends will continue and that, as a result, the economy will have to grow slowly. The balance of payments constraint will operate.

A temporary balance of payments problem

Although the sharp shift into deficit on the balance of payments was regarded as an unwelcome development by supporters of Mrs Thatcher's economic policies, they do not regard it in the same gloomy light as her critics. Former Chancellor of the Exchequer Nigel Lawson, when in office, claimed that a deficit on current account was not a problem as long as it could be easily financed. This, he said, was more easily achieved in a world of unrestricted capital movements. He also cited the case of Denmark, which had been running current account deficits since the 1950s. But, while this argument holds for small economies and, in the case of larger economies, for relatively short periods, it is probably not the case that a large industrial economy can run big deficits for years on end.

A stronger argument is that the deficit that emerged in the late 1980s was due to the failure of policy to control demand properly and was a temporary phenomenon. According to Professor Maynard: 'Although Britain's foreign trade problem in 1988 does not bear witness to the failure of the Government's supply side strategy, the government cannot be exculpated from allowing domestic demand to increase too fast in 1988.' In addition, he suggests, some of the deterioration in the current account position was due to the sharp rise in investment in the late 1980s, which resulted in a sharp rise in imports of capital goods. Such investment will generate economic growth, and exports, in the future.

The truth seems to lie somewhere in between the views of the critics and the supporters. The decline in the deficit in 1990 and 1991 showed that it was related, in part, to the strength of demand in the economy. However, there is also a longer-term problem, and the underlying position appears to be that, when economic growth is at its long-run average of around 2.5 per cent, the current account is likely to be in sizeable, and possibly increasing, deficit.

Mrs Thatcher's final acts

Finally, let us look at two events that occurred right at the very end of Mrs Thatcher's period in office. The first was the introduction (and under John Major subsequent abandonment) of the Community Charge or Poll Tax. The second was entry into the exchange rate mechanism of the European Monetary System in October 1990.

The Poll Tax

The **Poll Tax** helped bring down Mrs Thatcher. Her challenger for the Conservative leadership, Michael Heseltine, won support by promising to abolish it. It ran into several problems. In the first year of its operation in England and Wales, poll tax levels were 30 per cent higher than the equivalent bill for domestic rates. This was both because of inflation and inadequate funding by central government, and because local authorities chose the time of the tax's introduction to boost their spending. Non-payment levels were high, partly because the tax was targeted at many people who had not had to pay the rates (which was restricted to heads of household). Collection and administrative costs were high. Most importantly, the tax was widely thought of as grossly unfair. In 1991, after Mrs Thatcher had left office, John Major's government proposed a new **Council Tax** to replace the Poll Tax. This, like the rates, was related to properties, not people. Council Tax bills would be set on the basis of the size and location of properties – every house or flat would be put into one of seven bands for this purpose. The only concession to the principle of the Poll Tax was that people living alone would pay a reduced tax, equivalent to 75 per cent of the Council Tax paid by two or more living in a similar property.

Entering the European Exchange Rate Mechanism

In June 1989, Mrs Thatcher, attending a meeting of European Community leaders in Madrid, set out the conditions under which the pound would enter the exchange rate mechanism (ERM) of the European Monetary System. These conditions were mainly that Britain's inflation rate be equal to the average of countries in the ERM, around 4.5 per cent, and that the other big countries in the system have removed their remaining **exchange controls**. The second condition was satisfied by 1 July 1990 when France and Italy had removed their controls. But when membership occurred on 5 October 1990, Britain's inflation rate, at 10.9 per cent, was twice the ERM average. John Major, the Chancellor of the Exchequer at the time of entry, said that the inflation condition could be waived as long as there was a good prospect of future British inflation falling to the ERM average. Entry was, however, partly a political decision, because the government was keen to enter the ERM before the special European Community intergovernmental conference on **European Monetary Union** (EMU), which began in December 1990.

The question of Britain's membership of the ERM was a contentious one. Nigel Lawson, Chancellor from 1983 to 1989, pressed strongly for entry in 1985 but Mrs Thatcher said that Britain was not ready. In

1987 and 1988, he operated an unofficial target for the pound against the deutschmark of just below DM3, as a prelude to entry. However this policy ran into problems, and caused interest rates to be reduced more than they should have been. Sir Alan Walters, Mrs Thatcher's former personal economic adviser, criticized the ERM because, by targeting the exchange rate, Britain would lose control over interest rates.

The ERM had been operating since March 1979 when, on 5 October 1990, British entry was announced. Britain had been a member of the wider European Monetary System from the start – which involved, among other things, pooling of gold and foreign currency reserves in Europe – but had not joined the ERM. Entry was at a central rate of DM2.95 and on wide, 6 per cent, bands. This means that the theoretical range for the pound was from DM2.77 to DM3.13. The plan was to shift to the narrow bands, allowing a fluctuation of 2.25 per cent either side of the central rate (i.e. DM2.88 to DM3.02) in time.

In the first year, membership of the ERM operated successfully. Britain's interest rates (bank base rates) were reduced from 15 per cent to 10.5 per cent as inflation fell from 10.9 per cent to 4 per cent. Interest rates were reduced without causing pressure on the pound. Membership did not prevent exports from growing strongly.

Advocates of ERM membership say that it will maintain Britain's inflation rate at around the level of the best in Europe, particularly Germany. In the absence of devaluation, industry will be forced to compete with Europe, thus wage settlements and price increases will have to match European levels. They say it will help business by removing exchange rate uncertainty, and encourage foreign investment in Britain, particularly from outside the European Community. There is evidence in favour of all three of these claims.

Critics of the ERM say that the success of the first year of membership, and the fall in inflation and interest rates, was due to the severity of Britain's 1990–91 recession. They believe that entry, by delaying interest rate cuts between October 1990 and February 1991, made the recession more serious than it need have been.

More fundamentally, critics of ERM membership believe that, by reducing Britain's control over interest rates, economic policy will fail to achieve its objectives. This can operate in two ways. In the 1980s most ERM member countries achieved low inflation, but at the expense of high unemployment. One view of the system is that it allows Germany to prevent the deutschmark's natural rise against other European currencies. Countries such as France and Italy, in trying to hold their currencies against the deutschmark, have to accept higher interest rates and a slower rate of economic growth, than would otherwise be the case. According to this criticism, Britain joined a system which, in return for low inflation, will mean higher unemployment.

Another criticism comes from the opposite direction. Sir Alan Walters developed the '**Walters critique**'. If the ERM worked perfectly and the foreign exchange markets believed there were not going to be any currency devaluations or revaluations, then the most attractive currencies would be those offering the highest interest rates. These would also probably be the countries with the highest inflation rates. Thus, money would flow from low-inflation Germany and the Netherlands to high-inflation Spain and Italy. To keep their currencies from rising too fast Spain and Italy would have to cut their interest rates, but this would make their inflation problem worse. Germany and the Netherlands, in contrast, would have to raise their rates, making their already low inflation even lower. So, far from bringing about a *convergence* of inflation performance, the ERM could push countries further apart.

The best way of viewing Britain's membership of the ERM is in the context of the medium-term financial strategy of the early 1980s. Instead of the domestic monetary targets that operated then, there is an external target, in the form of the pound's ERM limits. Judging the success of membership will only be possible in the medium-term. The government believes that low inflation, if maintained, will stimulate strong economic growth, and that belonging to the ERM will help rather than hinder in that aim. The wider question of whether or not the ERM promotes economic convergence will also determine whether, over the next few years, the present European Monetary System evolves into full European Monetary Union, with a single currency and a European central bank setting monetary policy for the whole Community.

KEY WORDS

Community Charge	Poll Tax
Exchange rate mechanism	European Monetary System
Incentives	Collective bargaining
Union power	Sound money
Economic indicators	Privatization
Public sector borrowing requirement	Public sector debt repayment
Recession	Financial crowding out
Industrial relations	Productivity
De-regulated economic environment	Supply side
Internal balance	External balance
Current account	Council Tax
Exchange controls	European Monetary Union
Walters' critique	

Reading list

Bazen, S. and Thirlwall, T., *Deindustrialization*, Heinemann Educational, 1989.

Godley, W., 'The British economy during the Thatcher era', *Economics* (Journal of the Economics Association), winter 1989.

Healey, N. and Levačić, R., *Supply side economics*, 2nd edn, Heinemann Educational, 1992.

Hill, B., The *European Community*, Heinemann Educational, 1991

Johnson, C., *The economy under Mrs Thatcher*, 1979–90, Penguin Books, 1991.

Matthews, K., 'The UK economic renaissance', *Economics* (Journal of the Economics Association), autumn 1989.

Maynard, G., 'Britain's economic recovery', *Economics* (Journal of the Economics Association, autumn 1989.

NIESR, *The UK Economy*, Heinemann Educational, 1990.

Wells, J., 'The economy after ten years: stronger or weaker?', *Economics* (Journal of the Economics Association), winter 1989.

Essay Topics

1. During the 1980s, the UK's balance of trade in manufactured goods has moved from surplus into deficit. Explain why and discuss whether it matters. (Associated Examining Board, 1989)
2. There is no case for reducing the rate of inflation in the UK below the average rate prevailing in other advanced countries. Discuss. (University of Oxford Delegacy of Local Examinations, 1989)
3. 'The replacement of domestic rates by a Community Charge (poll tax), merely substitutes one inefficient tax for another.' Discuss. (University of London School Examinations Board, 1989)
4. On what basis do you think local government expenditure should be financed? (University of Cambridge Local Examinations Syndicate, 1989)
5. 'British membership of the European Exchange Rate Mechanism is a strategy designed to reduce the rate of inflation at the expense of domestic output and employment.' Discuss. (Oxford & Cambridge Schools Examination Board, 1991)

Data Response Question 5

Changes in UK international cost competitiveness in manufacturing
The graph below is based on information from the NIESR and the DTI and are reproduced from *NEDC British Industrial Performance*. Answer the following questions.
1. Define: relative labour costs; relative productivity; sterling

effective exchange rate; relative unit labour costs.
2. Explain the difference between labour costs and wage (or salary) costs.
3. (i) Account for the trend in relative productivity between 1976 and 1980.
   (ii) Does the chart confirm the view that there has been a 'productivity miracle' in the UK since 1980?
4. What factors influencing the competitiveness of the UK economy are *not* included in the chart?
5. What are the implications for the British economy of trends since 1981 in relative unit labour costs?

(Oxford & Cambridge Schools Examination Board, 1989)

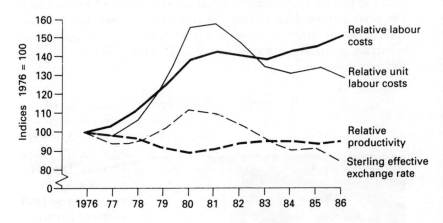

Chapter Seven

Conclusions

Mrs Thatcher's period in office, which ended in 1990, has provided a rich vein of material for those wishing to examine economic policy in practice. Many of the policy changes introduced in 1979 represented abrupt changes in direction; and, perhaps more than with any other post-war government, the aims were set out at the start and can easily be compared with the actual results.

Through a combination of accident and design, Mrs Thatcher has changed Britain's economic landscape, to the point where the clock can never be turned back to the old model of the 1960s and 70s. The interesting question is to what extent future governments – of whatever political persuasion – will seek to take the economy in a different direction.

THE LION, THE WITCH AND THE WARDROBE .

Index

Autumn Statement, 1986 31
Bacon, Robert 34
Balance of payments 82–84
Bank of England, 6, 12, 16
Beveridge report 48
Black economy 41, 45–46
Bretton Woods System 14, 15
British Gas 32
British Leyland 29
British Petroleum 33
British Steel Corporation 29
British Telecom 32
Broad money 7, 15
Brown, C.V. 43, 55–56
Budgets 49–51
   1979 Budget 1–2, 11, 39–40,
     49–57, 76
   1980 Budget 9
   1981 Budget 49, 76
   1984 Budget 45, 50
   1987 Budget 44
   1988 Budget 46, 49–50
   1989 Budget 49–50
   1990 Budget 49
Cambridge version of quantity
   theory 4–5, 15
Capital spending 31, 34
Chicago 3
Clegg, Hugh 11, 27
Closed shops 59, 62, 72
Confederation of British Industry 31
Conservative Party manifestoes 3,
   18, 25, 38, 57
Corporation tax 32, 45
Corset 7, 15
Credit controls 7, 15
Crowding out 19–22, 34, 79
Current spending 31, 34
Demand for money 5, 15
Direct taxation 38
Electrical, Electronic,
   Telecommunication and Plumbing
   Trades Union 70
Eltis, Walter 34

Employment Acts 1980 63
   1982 63–64
   1988 65
   1990 65
European Monetary System 13, 75,
   84, 85, 86, 87, 88
Externalities 23, 34
Fforde, John 12
Fine tuning 9, 15
Fiscal policy 7, 15, 18–56
Fisher, Irving 3–4, 15
Friedman, Milton 3, 5, 6, 8
Full employment 4–6, 15
GCHQ 63
Green Paper on Union Reform, 1987
   64–65, 72
Howe, Geoffrey 1, 2, 14, 39, 46
Income effect 42
Indifference curves 41–42
Indirect taxation 39
Industrial action 62–65, 67–70, 72,
   79
Inflation, 1980s' fall 13–15, 16, 80
Inflationary expectations 9, 14–16,
   73
Infrastructure 31, 34
Insider-outsider models 61
Institute for Fiscal Studies 45
International Monetary Fund 9, 25,
   26
Joseph, Keith 29
Keegan, William 15
Keynes, John Maynard 5, 8, 19
Keynesians 8, 15, 48
Laffer, A. 43–44
Lawson, Nigel 13, 14, 44–45, 55–56,
   70, 80, 84, 85
M0 5, 6, 13
M1 12
M3 10–13, 15
M4 13
M5 6, 7
Major, John 1, 14, 75, 84, 85
Medium-term financial strategy
   9–10, 15

Miners' strike 30, 69–70
Minford, P. 43, 48, 59–61, 77
Mixed economy 18, 34
Monetarism 2, 8–13, 15
Monetarists 3, 8, 15
Monetary policy, defined 7, 16
Monetary targets 9–11, 12–13, 15
Money supply 2–13, 15, 16
Morris, Derek 72
Narrow money 6, 15
National Coal Board 29, 69–70
National Economic Development
    Council 60
National Graphical Association 70
National Health Service 18, 23, 27,
    29, 66
National Institute 48
National Union of Mineworkers
    69–71
Natural monopolies 24
News International 70
North Sea Oil 1, 12, 25
Opportunity cost 42
Organization for Economic Co-
    operation and Development 30,
    52, 56
Pay boom 11
Petro-currency 12, 15
Pile, William 46
Poll Tax 40, 75, 84, 85
Postal ballots 64
Pound 1979–80 strength 11–12, as
    monetary target 13
Poverty trap 41, 46–47
Privatization 1, 20, 24, 31–34, 35,
    78
Progressive taxation 38
Pryke, Richard 23, 35
PSL2 12
Public expenditure
cuts 26–29, 77
survey and control 29–30
White Papers 26, 27
Public sector
size of 18–19, 24
relative efficiency of 22–24

borrowing requirement 10, 20, 34,
    35, 78
Quantity theory of money 3–8, 15
Regressive taxation 39
Relative price effect 25
Retention ratio 48
Riddell, Peter 30
Sandford, C 55–56
Sight deposits 10, 15
SOGAT '82, 70
Star Chamber 29
Sterling M3 10–15
Stock Exchange 32–34
Substitution effect 42
Supplementary special deposits
    scheme 7
Supply side 2, 38–56, 77, 81
Tax cuts 34, 38–56, 77
government's record on 49–52,
    55–56
and incentives 40–45
Thatcher, Margaret 1, 2, 7, 9, 11,
    13, 18, 20, 26, 28, 29, 30, 34, 39,
    40, 44, 46, 49, 51, 52, 58, 62, 65,
    66, 67, 68, 69, 71, 75, 90
Time
deposits 10, 15
lags 9, 15
Trade Union Act, 1984 64
Trade unions 57–74
development of 57–58
and pay 58–60
and employment 60–61
membership 65–67
Treasury 8, 9, 13, 19, 29, 30, 31, 33,
    40, 43, 50, 51, 77
Treasury and Civil Service
    Committee 8
Trustee Savings Bank 33
Unemployment 12, 29, 47–48, 66,
    68–69, 71–72, 73, 75, 79, 86
and productivity 71–72
Unemployment trap 41,47–48
Value added tax 11, 39–40, 46, 77
Velocity of circulation 4–8, 15
Wapping dispute 69–70